# PRAISE FOR JACKSON DEAN CHASE

— USA TODAY BESTSELLING AUTHOR —

AS SEEN IN

## BUZZFEED AND THE HUFFINGTON POST

"[Jackson Dean Chase is] a fresh and powerful new voice."
— Terry Trueman, Printz Honor author of *Stuck in Neutral*

"[Chase] grabs readers from page one."
— Nate Philbrick, author of *The Little One*

"[Jackson Dean Chase] succeeds in taking fiction to a whole new level."
— TheBaynet.com

"[Jackson's fiction is] diligently crafted…"
— The Huffington Post

"Irresistible… [Jackson knows how to write] a heart-pounding story full of suspense, romance, and action!"
— Buzzfeed

# WRITING GUIDES BY JACKSON DEAN CHASE

FAST, FUN ADVICE FOR TODAY'S BUSY AUTHOR

## NONFICTION

# WRITING APOCALYPSE AND SURVIVAL

## A MASTERCLASS IN POST-APOCALYPTIC SCIENCE FICTION AND ZOMBIE HORROR

### JACKSON DEAN CHASE

WWW.JACKSONDEANCHASE.COM

First Edition, July 2018

ISBN-13: 978-1722681746 / ISBN-10: 1722681748

Published by Jackson Dean Chase, Inc.

**WRITING APOCALYPSE AND SURVIVAL**

**PUBLISHER'S NOTE**

*For the end,*
*which is closer than you think.*

# WRITING APOCALYPSE AND SURVIVAL

# INTRODUCTION

DEATH HAS ALWAYS FRIGHTENED US, but it's normally on a personal level: losing family, friends, pets. When death looms larger than that—in war, for example—it becomes even more horrible. But still, we know life must go on. That is, until the nukes come out, or the bioweapons, the pandemics, the asteroids, even aliens or robots scorching the planet clean. Then we're not just talking about the death of millions. We're talking planet-wide extinction. The end of man.

Nothing personifies the end better than zombies. They give us time to reflect, to see death coming for us. They let us see what we become, and in some ways, what we have always been: parasitic organisms programmed to feed off death and off each other.

To quote my favorite line from *Dawn of the Dead* (1978):

"Every dead body that is not exterminated becomes one of them. It gets up and kills! The people it kills get up and kill!"

Zombies don't leave us any choice. They won't stop, so we can't. We have to keep fighting—and writing.

This book gives you the tools to destroy the world any way you want: from a mushroom cloud of revenge to ripped apart by undead savages. Any way you slice it, the Earth dies screaming.

— Jackson Dean Chase
*Get a free book at*
www.JacksonDeanChase.com

P.S.: Although there's plenty of advice about zombies inside, most of the information applies to writing *any* kind of apocalyptic or post-apocalyptic fiction—even regular disasters that don't end the world, like earthquakes or hurricanes. So if you're writing something like *The Road*, *The Day After Tomorrow*, or *Mad Max*, you'll still get a ton of value. You can easily swap out the word "zombies" and insert aliens, cannibals, mutants, robots, vampires, or hostile animals or humans. You may need to do a little tweaking, but it's not hard.

To make things easier, this "ultimate" edition adds chapters and advice on writing killer machines, mutants, and animals. For other enemies, refer to my best selling book, *Writing Monsters and Maniacs*.

In particular, I want to assure you that all my Plot Templates work *regardless* of whether you're writing zombies or not.

## PUBLISHER'S NOTE

This book was previously published as *How to Write Realistic Zombies and Post-Apocalyptic Fiction*. This "ultimate" edition has been newly revised and expanded with over 50 pages of exciting new content, including mutants and animals, killer machines, disasters, and two new apocalypse plot templates!

Some of the material in this book was previously published in *Gore Girls*, *How to Write Realistic Monsters, Aliens, and Fantastic Creatures* (now out of print), *Lost Girls*, *Post-Apocalypse Writers' Phrase Book*, *Writing Dynamite Story Hooks*, and *Writing Monsters & Maniacs* (all by Jackson Dean Chase). Some of this material has been revised for its appearance here.

# 3 STAGES OF THE APOCALYPSE

SOCIETAL COLLAPSE COMES IN STAGES. This chapter assumes your setting is a contemporary one. If your apocalypse takes place in the Wild West, the Middle Ages, or a Martian colony, you'll have to make some adjustments.

As I was writing this chapter, I realized that conditions in the apocalypse follow the famous Kübler-Ross grief cycle: Denial (Pre-Apocalypse), Anger and Bargaining (Apocalypse), Depression and Acceptance (Post-Apocalypse). When in doubt, the grief cycle can serve as a guideline to how your characters should be reacting to each stage. Of course, not all characters will be on the same grief cycle at the same time; some will process slower or faster than others.

With this chapter, I'm looking to strike the right balance between what makes a great fictional apocalypse and what happens in a real one. I may make certain assumptions you disagree with, and that's fine. It's your story, change what you want.

## ✓ PRE-APOCALYPSE CONDITIONS

The pre-apocalypse stage is defined as from the time the first known warning of the apocalypse appears. A few disturbing news reports begin to trickle in, but these are ignored or downplayed by traditional media outlets, who either fail to see the threat or actively try to suppress civilian knowledge by colluding with the government. They instead cover the latest celebrity breakup or political scandal as if those are more important than the potential end of humanity.

The warning begins to catch fire among "fringe" talk shows (radio, podcasts, etc.) and on social media. In a pandemic or zombie situation, videos of "sick people" will be shared, spreading fear. These videos will be downplayed or dismissed as hoaxes or drugged-out psychos like the infamous "Causeway Cannibal" who bit off a homeless man's face while allegedly high on bath salts. In your story, someone like this could be an escaped zombie from a secret government lab, or simply "Patient Zero," the first known case of the zombie virus.

While the top levels of government and military are informed of the potential threat to humanity, the general population is not. At first, everything is available at normal prices. The odds of you running into zombies or armed looters is almost non-existent.

As more wild rumors and reports begin to circulate, the mainstream media will begin to pay more attention to the crisis, legitimizing it. The 24/7 cable news cycle will feed the fear to rake in ratings profits; they will pass on government disinformation, out of date information, and anything that keeps eyeballs glued to screens. An endless live-stream of talking heads, self-proclaimed "experts" and "analysts" will spout platitudes, lies, conspiracy theories, and hate. They will focus on the wrong things and argue about them ferociously.

Facts are meaningless in a post-fact world; the only thing the majority of the public responds to are the calculated emotional pleas of dangerous demagogues; men who promise heaven and deliver hell. One or more of these con-men and future tyrants will spring up in every state, each with their own rabid band of followers. Some will be religious, some secular, but all will demand absolute obedience and group-think: "The leader knows best. Only he can save us."

In an effort to look more all-knowing and wise, the demagogues will blame others for the crisis and oncoming societal collapse: the blacks, the gays, Muslims, the Chinese, the Russians. They'll blame it on illegal immigrants sneaking disease, crime, and unrest past our borders. They'll blame it on sinners and atheists and anyone but themselves. Not them; their group is special. They've been chosen to survive and woe to anyone who gets in their way!

Survival supplies and trade goods will begin to sell out even as prices rise. There will be a run on the banks. Wall Street and world markets react accordingly. Riots flare up in urban areas; these may be brutally repressed or quarantined and left to "burn themselves out." Unless you're in a riot zone, the odds of running into zombies, infected, or armed looters rises, but is still relatively low.

Chatter among anarchists, separatists, survivalists, and para-military groups will increase as they sense the end is near. Having prepared for an extinction-level event like this for years, they will quickly and quietly retreat off the grid to their well-stocked "bug out" locations, taking whatever extra supplies they can beg, buy, borrow, or steal. These bug out locations could be an armed wilderness compound, a remote cabin, a bomb shelter, or anywhere defensible that isolates them from the rest of society. There they will continue to monitor the situation from a position of relative safety.

Once the government makes an announcement confirming the apocalyptic threat is unavoidable and/or declares martial law, the pre-apocalypse stage ends. The government will almost certainly lie about being close to finding a solution, hoping to trick civilians into remaining obedient long enough for the government to get a handle on things. They will not disclose the true or complete nature and severity of the threat until it is too late, if at all.

In the face of an increasingly oppressive regime, eventually, everyone rebels. Mass panic and civil unrest explode, and while some riots will be stamped out, many won't.

The apocalypse begins!

## ✓ APOCALYPSE CONDITIONS

The apocalypse hits cities first and hardest, as too many people with too few survival skills all make similar bad decisions at the same time. Infected or rioting neighborhoods will be cordoned off by police, national guard, and/or the military. Hospitals will be jammed and become deathtraps, as will freeways. It will be almost impossible to escape the cities unless you can access boats or helicopters.

The stock market crashes and ceases trading. Banks shutter and refuse to allow withdrawals. Riots spread and are no longer restricted to urban areas. Whole neighborhoods go up in flames or are lost to violence. The odds of running into zombies, infected, or armed looters is high. Everyone is angry, everyone is scared, trying to make some kind of last minute bargain with God or anyone who will listen. Enterprising criminals take advantage of this to offer "protection" in exchange for crazy demands that seem less and less crazy as days go by and conditions worsen.

The media and internet becomes increasingly alarmist, painting a bloody picture of the end as it happens, city by city, state by state. Viewers are barraged by non-stop footage of rampaging zombie hordes devouring people in the streets, bloodthirsty looting, and the military executing civilians (the infected, the criminal, the curfew breakers). The Emergency Broadcast System interrupts the news with out-of-date lists of civil defense shelters and with warnings to stay in your homes and trust the government.

People in small towns and rural areas band together, setting up road blocks to keep sick people, looters, and strangers out. A local militia is established and/or extra citizens deputized. The people pool resources. They hunker down and pray. The smaller the town and more remote the area, the better chances they have, but even this will not save them. Someone always gets careless, someone always tries to cheat. And people die. Only in the case of a zombie apocalypse, they don't stay dead, so any fight, any wound or disease, even old age is another chance for the zombie virus to pop up inside supposedly safe, sealed borders.

Meanwhile, the wealthy and larger corporations will sequester themselves and their people in their remote estates or facilities. They will have the resources to stockpile supplies even at the rapidly escalating (and utterly insane)—at least until everyone realizes that paper money is going to be worthless, which happens all too soon.

At this point, the barter system is back, and only fools will trade for paper money, stocks, bonds, or other worthless securities. Their value can no longer be guaranteed. The only things that have value now are things that help you survive, or at least make surviving more pleasant.

Seats of power within local, state, and federal government will tighten security as they try to maintain order. High-ranking officials, their families, and senior staff will be hustled into secret bunkers where they will bicker amongst themselves, issuing increasingly contradictory, illegal, and inhumane orders that do more harm than good.

At their behest, a variety of (mostly) ill-timed and poorly conceived military operations will go into effect aimed at stamping out human and/or zombie resistance by creating "safe zones." Sick people will be shot on sight or rounded up and herded like cattle to what will inevitably become death camps.

Many citizens will be forcibly evacuated to FEMA camps; those who resist are beaten, cuffed, or shot. In a plague or zombie scenario, someone is going to secretly be infected and not tell anyone, fearing what will happen. Somehow, they'll get past the medical inspection and hide their illness as long as they can. Then they infect others in the camp. Or, maybe the government is using the camps to test out experimental vaccines. These vaccines fail and turn those injected into zombies—perhaps even mutant, intelligent ones.

Prisons are another possible setting for the government to test vaccines as they did in *Z Nation* (TV, 2014-present).

The military will eventually abandon camps and areas deemed "non-essential" or indefensible. Some will go rogue and refuse to follow orders once they see which way the wind is blowing; these elements will hole up in their bases to "wait it out" or take over a more desirable area under pretense of martial law.

Even within loyal units, morale will waiver, schism, and crack between those who believe they can stay the course, and those who see no point in getting themselves and their buddies killed in an unwinnable and apparently endless war.

Elite special ops units are more likely to remain loyal to their government and/or service branch, at least to the point when they perceive all is lost. Elite units that stick together operate much the same as rogue military, commandeering whatever they can talk or force people out of. These men are battle-hardened professional soldiers armed with the best weapons, body armor, and spy tech. That makes them power players wherever they go. Whether they choose to use that power for good, selfish, or evil ends is up to them.

While I have little faith in politicians, before I paint too grim a picture of the police and military response, it's important to note that I believe the majority of men and women serving in our armed forces and law enforcement are good people who believe in law and order, liberty, and defending our way of life. They are service-oriented and want to give back by defending our country from internal or external threats. But there's always one bad apple in every unit or department. Just like there's one in every office or classroom. And all it takes is one to mess things up.

*And that's on a good day.*

During the apocalypse, these bad apples will get innocent civilians killed. They'll get their squad buddies killed. They'll spread lies and half-truths and whisper dissent. They will corrupt morale and crush hope. They'll insist their ideas are right, that there's no point following orders when they could do so much better on their own. If they manage to sway a few key people to their side, that's when every-thing falls apart.

Maybe this is too cynical or grim, but remember, this is fiction we're talking about, and great fiction thrives on conflict. It needs bad people doing bad things. It needs villains and cowards and fools to make your heroes stand out.

## THE POWER GRID

At some point during the apocalypse, certain areas will lose power either permanently or as intermittent outages. In *The Walking Dead*, electricity and running water are readily available in many areas even years after the zombies take over. But with no one left to maintain the utilities, they must give out eventually. It's up to you whether you want to keep the lights and internet working after civilization falls, and for how long they remain.

## THE NUCLEAR OPTION

Not every apocalypse is a nuclear one, but for those that are, you'll need to know what happens when you drop a nuke on a city or other area: the fireball radius, the air blast radius, the thermal radiation radius, and estimated number of fatalities. Wouldn't be nice if there was an app for that? One you could customize not only by location, but by how many bombs hit, and even what type they were?

While researching this book I just happened to find such an app, and it's fantastic!

- http://nuclearsecrecy.com/nukemap/

In seconds, it lets you detonate every type of nuclear weapon from around the world, from the tiniest 20-ton "Davy Crockett" to the largest 100-megaton "Tsar Bomba."

If you're going nuclear, take a look at *The Day After* (TV, 1983), *Testament* (1983), *Miracle Mile* (1988), and *Jericho* (TV, 2006-2008). Also consider a nuclear power reactor meltdown like Three Mile Island, Chernobyl, or Fukushima.

What about weird fallout from a bioweapon strike or testing accident? In the novel, *One Rainy Night* (1991), author Richard Laymon imagines a weird black rain falling over a town. Whoever gets soaked by it becomes a homicidal maniac until the "rain" is washed off.

Meanwhile, in the real world, clear blobs of toxic "star jelly" fell from the sky over Oakville, Washington in 1994, sickening and killing locals. The still unexplained incident was profiled on *Unsolved Mysteries* (TV, 1987-2002).

Or, instead of nukes, what about war? You could set your story during the invasion of a hostile foreign power: *Red Dawn* meets *Dawn of the Dead*.

## OTHER WAYS TO MAKE IT WORSE

If you want to make things even crazier for your story, have the apocalypse strike during a natural disaster like Hurricane Katrina, as Joe McKinney did in his novel, *Dead City* (2006).

What about during a massive earthquake? Watch *Earthquake* (1974) and read *Quake* (1974) by Rudolph Wurlitzer or *Quake* (1995) by Richard Laymon for non-zombie earthquake apocalypse novels.

Other disaster options would be to have characters trapped in a burning skyscraper like *The Towering Inferno* (1974) or a mountain resort like *Avalanche* (1978).

*The Road* (2009) doesn't explain its apocalypse, leaving viewers to guess at what the cold, ashen landscape means: nuclear winter, asteroid impact, climate change? Who knows? Like not explaining how zombies exist, not explaining your apocalypse has a certain elegance. It also means never having to apologize for getting the science wrong.

If you want to go more sci-fi, what about an extinction level event, such as a meteor or asteroid strike? In *Where Have All the People Gone* (TV, 1974), a solar flare turns people to dust. Radiation from a passing comet does the same in *Night of the Comet* (1984), with the added benefit of turning some survivors into zombies.

If you're not into natural disasters, what about setting your apocalypse during a blackout, either localized or nationwide, such as from an electro-magnetic pulse (EMP)? To see what happens in an urban environment, research the 1977 New York City blackout and watch *Blackout* (1978). For a rural setting, try *The Trigger Effect* (1996).

Best selling author James Herbert imagined several apocalypse scenarios in his novels. In *The Fog* (1975), a toxic cloud from the center of the earth turns everyone who breathes it into homicidal maniacs. In *The Dark* (1980), a demonic cloud of living darkness does pretty much the same thing. In *Domain* (1984), mutant rats attack survivors of a nuclear war; and in *'48* (1996), at the end of World War II, the defeated Nazis unleash a bioweapon that kills most of humanity.

Unusual shelter locations can provide great atmosphere for your story. The most famous example is the shopping mall in *Dawn of the Dead* (1978 and 2004 remake), but there are all kinds of locations more exotic than that. In *Day of the Dead* (1985), a civilian science team and its military escort hunker down in a former mine shaft converted into an underground storage facility. Thomas Koloniar has a Green Beret team embed themselves in a missile silo in his novel, *Cannibal Reign* (2012).

Wherever your survivors are going to ride out the apocalypse, make sure it has advantages and disadvantages, including one major flaw through which your villains and monsters invade. At the right time, of course.

The apocalypse is all about timing.


## ✓ POST-APOCALYPSE CONDITIONS

Now we arrive at the end, which is really the beginning: the new, nightmare world where only the strong survive. But for how long?

This is *The Road Warrior* world where anything goes and might makes right. Your chance of running into zombies is extremely high, especially the closer you get to cities. Almost the same as your odds of encountering armed looters, rogue military, biker gangs, petty tyrants, cults, crazies, infected, and other desperate scum who want to deprive you of life, liberty, and the pursuit of happiness. There are still good people out there, but unless they have banded together and armed themselves, they exist only as victims or potential victims.

Goods and services are now on a strictly barter basis, although to those who still find value in them, precious metals, gems, and jewelry may be traded in lieu of anything else.

Power and running water may be available, but not in all areas. A last few media and internet holdouts may be broadcasting information, but are unlikely to last long. One by one, these voices will fade until only static remains.

Survivors must go through a grieving process where they mourn their old life and not all will find the will to go on in this mad world. There were a lot of suicides during the apocalypse, but there will be many more now, once people realize the old world is never coming back and this nightmare is all there is. Depression and post-traumatic stress syndrome (PTSD) from the horrors these people have gone through will take their toll.

Others may see a a chance to prove themselves and find the strength not just to get by day to day, but to thrive. These individuals provide a slim beacon of hope, though they'll need more than optimism to survive. They'll need a plan. And likely another plan, and another, as they find their hopes dashed one by one—by the living or the dead.

Survivors will naturally divide into loners, small bands, or large groups. The best of these will have a few jack of all trades but also contain skilled specialists: leader/diplomat, medic, mechanic, scout, and soldier. If you're familiar with games like *Dungeons & Dragons*, this is similar to putting together a balanced adventuring party with a cleric, fighter, thief, and wizard. Some groups may have an oddball who isn't necessary for survival, but adds enough value to keep around (a gourmet chef, for example).

Tiny pockets of civilization remain, but won't last long unless they are militarized with strong defenses. With militarization comes confidence, a cause to believe in, but that can quickly turn to arrogance and a desire to apply a military solution to problems better solved through diplomacy. Rushing to war will destroy some of these communities and send survivors into the wild to start over.

Eventually, given strong walls and capable leaders, some of the more level-headed outposts will band together in a loose association for commerce and defense, perhaps aligning into a federation strong enough to exterminate or drive off the human predators lurking outside their walls. Within these communities, jobs exist, but not the old jobs. These are jobs that make sense in this new world. Everyone must contribute. Those who cannot or will not are banished or killed. This is the new reality: *Be useful or be dead.*

## THE POST-APOCALYPSE JOB MARKET

Assuming your story takes place in a post-apocalypse world years after societal collapse, and assuming some semblance of civilization has returned, then certain skills are going to be in demand. Here's a list of hot jobs in alphabetical order:

- Architect/Construction/Engineer/Welder
- Agriculture/Farming
- Appliance/Electronics Repair
- Blacksmith/Bladesmith
- Doctor/Nurse/Pharmacist/Veterinarian
- Firearm Manufacture and Repair
- HAM Radio Expert
- Hunter/Scout
- Irrigation/Well Construction
- Leatherworker
- Mechanic
- Midwife
- Prostitute
- Security Services/Self-Defense Training
- Sewing/Tailoring/Textile Manufacture
- Soap/Candle Manufacturer
- Teacher

Notice banker, bureaucrat, CEO, lawyer, politician, and Wall Street crook did not make the list. Unfortunately for me, neither did author.

## MOST VALUABLE TRADE GOODS

With the death of Wall Street and the banks comes the end of currency as we know it. The world returns to the barter system. Goods and services are the new wealth, but such wealth is limited to what you can keep or carry. Walled communities will be able to hoard more of this "wealth," making them attractive places to visit, but also to attack.

Although some survivalists scoff at hoarding gold and silver because "you can't eat it," that doesn't change the fact that people have always loved the stuff and have used it as currency through one societal collapse after another.

Here's a list of the most valuable trade goods in alphabetical order:

- Animals, Guard and Hunting
- Animals, Livestock
- Backpacks/Personal Storage
- Body Armor
- Books ("how to" manuals)
- Bow/Crossbow and Ammunition
- Camping/Hiking Gear
- Cloth and Clothing (durable, warm, and waterproof)
- Crowbar
- Firearms and Ammunition (common calibers)
- Firewood
- Food, Fresh
- Food, Preserved
- Fuel (Gasoline, Oil, etc.)
- Maps
- Medicine
- Luxury Goods (alcohol, cigarettes, etc.)
- Personal Defense (tasers, pepper spray, etc.)
- Pesticide
- Precious Gems, Jewelry, and Metals
- Seeds (non-GMO)

- Sewing Kits and Supplies
- Solar Power
- Specialty Items *
- Spices
- Toiletries/Personal Hygiene Products
- Tools
- Vehicles
- Vitamins
- Water
- Water Filtration
- Weapons, Modern (explosives, firearms, etc.)
- Weapons, Primitive (axes, bows, knives, spears, swords, etc.)

* Specialty Items cover anything of high value to a specific profession or group that most people have little to no use for. Stockpiling them is a risk few survivors will undertake unless they can reasonably expect to unload the goods sooner rather than later.

For example, biohazard and radiation specialty items would include disinfectants, Geiger counters, hazmat suits, medical grade particulate masks, and potassium iodide pills. If your world was nuked or exposed to a bio-weapon, some or all of these items might switch from specialty items to being in high demand for almost everyone. Otherwise, they have limited use, like if you were going to try and restart a nuclear power plant or to look for a zombie vaccine in a biological research facility.

# 2

## SURVIVING THE END

MANY PEOPLE FIND SURVIVING a normal day in our modern world challenging; now throw societal collapse and a horde of zombies, cannibals, or mutants into the mix and see what happens! Some people are going to kill themselves, some are going to experience temporary or permanent mental illness, and others are going to find a way to fight through the horror.

### SEVEN STEPS TO SURVIVE

There's a short list of actions all survivors need to take right off the bat: just seven steps. The exact order they should be followed in change based on the circumstances your character finds himself in at the beginning of the apocalypse. If he already has a viable shelter with food, water, heat, electricity, and warm clothes, then collecting weapons and fortifying his shelter come first. Once he's done that, he can begin to worry about how he's going to solve the rest.

1. Find food and water.
2. Get weapons (ranged and melee).
3. Protect yourself from the elements.

4. Find shelter.
5. Fortify your area or use natural barriers.
6. Plan your long-term strategy.
7. Find a group to help you survive.

### ✓ Step 1: Find Food and Water

You need to stay hydrated. Who knows when the water might be shut off or contaminated?

1. Fill up every container you can.
2. Fill all sinks and bathtubs.
3. Set out containers to collect rainwater.

Food is energy. You need energy to defend yourself. That means your food supply is critical. You need to:

1. Ration the food you have.
2. Freeze food that might go bad (if possible).
3. Any food that is perishable and can't be frozen should be eaten first.
4. Create farming opportunities.

Urban farming opportunities could be a rooftop or fenced garden to provide fresh spices and veggies. Rural farming opportunities include the possibility of not only a larger and more diverse crop of veggies, but harvesting meat and dairy from livestock.

If you have to venture out to get food and water, make sure to take a weapon and plan several alternate routes to and from your destination since roads could be blocked, bad guys running wild, etc.

Once you locate a grocery store:

1. Get as much water as you can.
2. Get as many non-perishable food items as you can.
3. Get any medicines you think you'll need.

4. Get at least one first aid kit.

5. Get toiletries/personal hygiene products.

6. Get a map of the state and your area.

7. Get any other supplies you think you'll need.

8. Get some portable entertainment items (books, etc.).

## ✓ Step 2: Get weapons (Ranged and Melee)

Every home has *some* kind of weapon: a kitchen knife, knitting needle, baseball bat, golf club, etc. A broken table or chair leg works as a club. You could even use a broken bottle, or if you're truly desperate, a shard of glass (preferably wrapped around the bottom to create a safe handle).

Most people can quickly lay hands on one of these basic melee weapons for close-combat. While clubs are a good choice (particularly against zombies), knives offer the most versatility. They're also lighter and easier to conceal.

One myth I'd like to bust is that you should "never bring a knife to a gunfight." That's only true if the enemy has his gun drawn, aimed, and is far enough away to use it before you can get to him. If his weapon is holstered or slung over the shoulder, and he's within seven yards, he may not have time to draw it, let alone aim it before the enemy runs up and stabs him. Even an untrained enemy with a knife is an absolute and immediate danger, both to firearms experts and martial arts masters alike.

In his controversial book, *Put 'Em Down, Take 'Em Out: Knife Fighting from Folsom Prison*, Don Pentacost detailed how a "prison yard rush" by an attacker with a knife will kill better-armed or skilled opponents almost every time, or at least result in multiple stab wounds before the attacker is stopped.

The other big myth is in thinking of an attack as a knife "fight." It's not a fight, it's attempted murder. Unless the attacker is a complete fool or trying to ward you off, you are not going to see the knife coming. He will not show it to you and invite you to a duel. The last thing he wants is a fair fight! If he can get behind you, he'll grab your head, tilt it back, then slit your throat. If he thinks you won't expect it, he'll casually walk by, stick the blade in you, and keep on going. You'll be dying before you even realize what happened. Or, he'll just rush up and stab the shit out of you as fast as he can.

Ranged weapon choices include firearms, air pistols, bows or crossbows, molotov cocktails, slingshots, rocks, etc. A homemade short-range flamethrower can be improvised with a lighter and bottle of hairspray. A pot of boiling water or coffee could burn or blind an attacker. Not to mention insect poison spray or bathroom cleaner squirt bottles; those are great for blinding enemies *and* they're easy to use without injuring yourself—plus, you get multiple shots.

With firearms, untrained users are unlikely to be accurate, but that doesn't mean they still can't hit a man-sized target. Just probably not wherever they were aiming for. It will take time for new users to adjust to the unexpected kick of their weapon when it fires; this also affects accuracy.

One more thing: It's vital to point out that being familiar with one type of gun or knife does not make you an expert with all of them. Each model is different.

### ✓ Step 3: Protect yourself from the elements

Most modern clothing sucks. It's cheap and not meant to last long. To survive the post-apocalyptic world, you need durable, warm, and waterproof clothes like Gortex, leather jackets, denim, etc. These materials are relatively zombie-proof, as well. Helmets, scarves, gloves, and boots protect from bites and scratches on areas that are weak points for many survivors.

### ✓ Step 4: Find shelter

If you have a shelter, is it the *right* one? Not necessarily for the rest of your life, but for right now. If you don't have shelter, find one fast. Bad guys and zombies are going to be everywhere soon. In a martial law situation, military or law enforcement might arrest or shoot you if you're caught out after curfew.

A fenced-in parking lot may not keep out bad guys, but should protect you from zombies. A vehicle makes a fine mobile shelter as long as the windows and fuel hold out. If you can't get inside a vehicle, you could hide under it. You could climb a tree or fire escape. You could hide in or behind a dumpster (just don't trap yourself in a dead end alley).

Storage unit facilities can make excellent shelters thanks to the fenced lot, password-protected entry gate, and limited number of people who can gain access. You can clear out the junk in units to block off the entrances. Chances are good you'll find a mattress you can sleep on as well as a variety of reading material. Looters may eventually target these facilities, but since the contents are a crap-shoot, they're more likely to target businesses where they know they can get what they want. In an apocalypse, the idea of "one-stop shopping" becomes more important than ever.

When seeking shelter, look for a place that's nondescript to avoid attracting attention. It should be away from the main streets but not too far from routes out of the area.

In a zombie apocalypse, avoid taking shelter in hospitals, doctor's offices, schools, churches, or public gathering places. These are some of the first places to be overrun. Despite having a high concentration of armed survivors, police stations and sheriff's offices are no safer. Officers responding to attacks are likely to be bitten, suspects may be infected, and it's only a matter of time until the bullets start flying. Do you want to be there when that happens?

### ✓ Step 5: Fortify your area or use natural barriers

Board up doors and windows. Leave yourself an opportunity to see out: don't cover peepholes or block off all access to windows unless absolutely necessary. If you run out of boards, break up some wooden furniture or cabinets. Still running short or need extra reinforcement? Push some heavy bookcases, tables, or mattresses into place.

If you're in a single-story residence with an elevated entrance, can you saw off the entry stairs? That won't stop determined humans, but will keep zombies from knocking on your door.

The staircases in a multi-level house or apartment building provides a second line of defense in case the ground floor is breached. You can block off the stairs to buy yourself time to escape to the roof or jump out a window.

In a multi-story shelter, prioritize securing the ground floor first (as well as basements with outside access). If you have any leftover boards, you should keep them on hand in case you need to shore up ground floor defenses. Boarding the upstairs windows is only necessary if bad guys can gain easy access via a nearby tree or neighbor's rooftop. Otherwise, you'll want to keep one or more upstairs windows free in case you need to use them to escape.

Keep the lights off or low! Stay away from windows. You don't want to be seen by any passers by (living or undead).

Obvious external fortifications announce your presence to the outside world like a big red flashing light. Unless you have a large, well-armed group, it's probably better not to block off the street with cars or build a guard tower in your backyard. The zombies won't care, but the bad guys will. After all, if you're going to all this trouble to keep them out, you must have some tasty stuff worth stealing...

If your shelter is in an insecure area, at some point, you will need to abandon it. Make a "bug out" plan for that and where you will go. The longer you wait to leave, the more you need to realize:

1. The world outside is getting more dangerous; and
2. All the good stuff (or at least the easiest) has been looted.

If you're in a wilderness setting, use natural barriers to reduce the number of ways an enemy can approach. While a campfire and hot meal might make you feel better, it also draws attention. Smoke can be seen from miles away. Fire or not, set up a series of tripwire alarms around your camp to warn when someone is approaching. You can do this by stringing noisy objects to the wires.

## ✓ Step 6: Plan your long-term strategy

Once you have found and fortified your shelter, you have time to think. However, that time is limited by your ability to defend yourself and how much food and water you have. Even if you have plenty for now, you don't know what problems the next day, even the next minute, might bring. Government forces could be coming to round you up. Armed looters could target your hideout. Or a zombie horde could sniff you out and surround you. Even if they can't get in, you can't get out. You may starve to death or die of dehydration before they go away.

Use your time wisely. Consider all your options, keeping emotions out of your decision-making. Dismiss ideas that are too ambitious or rely on others outside your current group. Always have a back-up plan in case things go wrong.

If you're in the city, plan to get out. If you're in the country, plan to get to the most remote and defensible location you can find. Either way, be prepared for others to have had the same idea and to have already beaten you there.

## ✓ Step 7: Find a group to help you survive

Joining a group is something almost every survivor must do at some point. On the surface, it makes sense. There is safety in numbers and groups provide for your social needs as well as your physical ones. You don't have to face the horrors of the apocalypse alone. But it's not just about finding a group, it's about finding the *right* group. Joining the wrong one can be more dangerous than going it alone.

Find out as much about the group as you can *before* and *after* you approach them. Shadow them; see how they treat each other and the people they meet. How effective are they are at scavenging supplies and killing enemies? Are they generous or cruel? Chances are, that's how they'll treat you.

If the group you approach is not immediately suspicious of you, that's a red flag. Either they have not adjusted to the new reality brought on by the apocalypse, or they have already sized you up as a victim. An overly-friendly group is likely to rob you, kill you, or worse. Keep an eye on the whole group, not just the ones you're talking to. If you see some circling behind you, you're in trouble. That may just be a wise precaution on their part, or else they are closing a trap. By the time you figure out which, it may be too late.

Don't assume a group will take you in just because you're human and "we're all in this mess together." They may only accept those who demonstrate some valuable skill or characteristic, or they could cling to old prejudices. They may simply not want to take on members outside their immediate friends and family. This does not make them bad people. If the group is neutral or reasonably friendly given the circumstances, tell them you understand and use the opportunity as a chance to exchange information or trade goods and services before you move on.

## THE THING ABOUT GROUPS

One of the main criticisms of zombie stories in general and *The Walking Dead* in particular is just how dumb some of the groups act. While ordinary civilians can be expected to make their fair share of mistakes, this should not happen when their group contains members trained in combat, security, and survival.

Since it's beyond the scope of this book to cover how every possible combination of civilians might act, I'm going to focus on the four types most likely to lead and survive: military and law enforcement, and preppers and survivalists.

## MILITARY AND LAW ENFORCEMENT

Having a character with a military or law enforcement background means the most common security errors never get made. That is, unless the character in question is one of the reckless or lazy "bad apples" discussed in the previous chapter. Then all bets are off.

Military or law enforcement characters will implement a "buddy system," so nobody ever goes anywhere without backup—and a weapon. Every character (who isn't obviously insane) will be provided with a weapon and shown how to use and care for it. For example, if it's a gun, how to clear a room, how to keep your finger off the trigger and to never point it at anyone you don't intend to shoot. How to field strip it. If it's a hammer or a club, how much room you need to swing it so you don't hit your buddy in the face.

On top of these basics will be training how to use the weapons in different situations (for example, against humans vs. harder to kill opponents such as zombies). In a zombie apocalypse, you can bet they will teach a "brain buster" protocol that shows how to prevent slain human opponents from coming back to life as zombies. After all, it's no good to kill someone who is only going to get back up a few minutes later and attack you all over again. You have to make sure they stay dead.

*The only good zombie is a dead zombie.*

When a group led by military or law enforcement approaches a building where the occupancy is unknown, and assuming they have at least a three-person team, the building will be presumed to be held by hostiles. The first team member bangs on the door, standing to its side so he can't be hit or surprised by anyone on the other side. Two more will crouch back and to either side, ready to provide covering fire or prevent any snipers from aiming out a window. Any resistance or refusal to answer the knock will be met with force; a locked door will be broken down, an unlocked door thrown open. The team will enter the building and proceed to sweep it clear, room by room. If the team has extra members, these may be stationed to cover the front and rear of the building. Their role is to prevent any hostiles from escaping and to keep the team's escape routes open should the mission go bad.

Military personnel know you don't waste ammo on an impossible fight; you beat a strategic retreat and save your bullets for whoever gets in your way. You do not stop or turn around and shoot at whatever is coming after you, especially is it's slow-moving zombies unlikely to catch you. That's a great way to get yourself and your buddies killed. What if you trip? What if you need those bullets later?

And yet time after time, we see characters who should know better make these exact same mistakes!

There's also no shooting at zombies from a moving vehicle. That's because shots from a moving vehicle are already likely to miss people. How much harder do you think it will be to hit a zombie when only head shots count?

Ammo checks will be frequent and accurate before, during, and after fights. Everyone loads, everyone reloads. Nobody is allowed to walk around with just the bullets in their gun; they are going to have at least enough to reload once or twice. When writing gun scenes, keep track of the bullets! Make sure the characters stop to reload. Not only is this realistic, but it gives you a chance to break up the action a little bit.

Finally, no group run by someone with a military or law enforcement background would allow a member to run or wander off for selfish or silly reasons. The buddy system, remember? And more than that, this is the apocalypse! You want to get yourself killed, that's your business. There's no splitting the group up to chase after someone who's acting like an idiot. That gets everyone dead, so the group is better off without them.

With military and law enforcement characters, the mission is the priority, whether it's scavenging for food or scouting an enemy base. Once people deviate from mission parameters, once they cease to follow orders, discipline breaks down. Things go south in a hurry.

There will always be scouting and surveillance with a military or law enforcement character in charge; the group will never rush blindly into a situation they have no intelligence on as Rick's group did with disastrous results in Season Six of *The Walking Dead*. It turns out "The Saviors" Rick's group killed weren't just a dozen bandits but part of a much larger, deadlier group. Likewise, military or law enforcement characters will always have an exit strategy and a rendezvous point.

A guard schedule and watch perimeter will be established and maintained around the group's camp or shelter. Guards will be trained what to watch out for and instructed not to be lured beyond the perimeter; they are to alert others in the group of any threat, preferably without calling attention to themselves and giving away their position to the enemy. When possible, a guard will take up watch in an elevated post that allows a 360-degree view of his surroundings, and he will maintain that field of vision, not just stare off in one direction with his back turned. Remember in *The Walking Dead*, Season Two, Episode One ("What Lies Ahead"), when Dale was on top of his RV with binoculars *and* a scoped rifle, yet somehow magically failed to see the zombie mega-herd coming until it was too late? That won't happen if military and law enforcement people are present.

When someone in the group proves incapable of obeying orders, they get reprimanded. They get punished. If that doesn't correct the problem, then they're out of the group. There's no time for babysitting troublemakers and morons when the world is falling apart. Military and law enforcement characters know this. They're here to help, they *want* to help, but if you can't help yourself, there's nothing they can do.

While military characters come with a number of impressive survival advantages, they do suffer one potentially fatal flaw: The tendency to blindly stick with any plan that has worked in the past, at least until it is proven that the enemy has not only caught on to it, but taken appropriate countermeasures. This failure to change and adapt can quickly translate into a high number of friendly casualties. Sometimes even then, these characters remain stubborn, failing to adapt to changing battlefield conditions.

To get a feel for how military characters might act in a war zone, watch *Apocalypse Now* (1979), *Platoon* (1986), *Full Metal Jacket* (1987), *Blackhawk Down* (2001), and *Tears of the Sun* (2003).

For a concise, well-researched sourcebook on creating realistic military and law enforcement characters, I highly recommend *Armed Professions: A Writer's Guide* by Clayton J. Callahan (2016).

For tips on writing realistic violence, check out *Violence: A Writer's Guide* (Second Edition, 2013) by Rory Miller, and my own *Post-Apocalypse Writers' Phrase Book* (2015).

## PREPPERS AND SURVIVALISTS

Characters with prepper or survivalist backgrounds will be able to lay hands on a ready stash of wisely hoarded supplies, or else be in a better position to acquire one. They will know which things are worth taking, which ones aren't, and why. Remember, most survivors are limited to what they can wear or carry. Excess weight slows you down and gets you killed or left behind.

Survivalists may know which plants and berries are safe to eat, how to hunt wild game, and which signs warn animals, humans, or zombies are nearby.

Both are likely to have a safe and secure well-stocked shelter in a remote location, from a hunting cabin to an underground bunker.

It's important to point out that although a lot of people use the terms prepper and survivalist interchangeably, they represent two different mindsets and skill sets (obviously with some overlap). Preppers typically plan for a *specific* foreseeable disaster, such as a tornado or nuclear war. Therefore, their plans vary greatly; some may only have enough supplies to last a few weeks, while some will have enough for months or years. Preppers prefer to gather in likeminded groups or communities. Prepping becomes a lifestyle for them, perhaps with gardening organic vegetables or other healthy, self-sufficient choices. For examples of people prepping for different types of disasters, take a look at *Doomsday Preppers* (TV, 2012-2014).

Unlike preppers, survivalists tend to be loners. While some focus on creating a permanent shelter for themselves and possibly a few others, they rarely have much interest in saving anyone outside close friends and loved ones. Also unlike most preppers, they train to be able to survive in one or more terrain types under difficult conditions. Think Bear Grylls of *Man vs. Wild* (TV, 2006-2011) or Les Stroud of *Survivorman* (TV, 2004-present). Note that just because a survivalist knows how to live off one terrain type, doesn't automatically mean he knows how to survive in others.

Survivalists are the most likely—and most dangerous—type of survivor to be encountered alone. They will be suspicious, if not openly hostile to strangers. Although unlikely to invite you into their shelter, they may be open to sharing information or trading goods and services. However, some are so paranoid they will want to kill you simply for knowing their location. Which, when you think about it, is not an entirely unreasonable reaction. While they may trust that *you* won't come back, they have no way to know who you might tell—especially under torture.

Note that if you see one survivalist, there's likely a second hiding nearby, and you can bet he's pointing his rifle at you.


## SURVIVOR PSYCHOLOGY

You can't live through the apocalypse without being traumatized. Watching your loved ones shot, stabbed, ripped apart, or worse, being infected and then coming back to life, is bound to take its toll on you. Attachments to others are dangerous in a world where people die every day in one horrible way or another. It only stands to reason that survivors are likely to develop a number of temporary or permanent mental illnesses as "coping skills," such as delusions, OCD, and post-traumatic stress disorder. It's one thing to go through a war, but what is it like to live in one that lasts forever? Because that's what the post-apocalypse world is: War against man. War against zombies. War against nature. War against yourself and your own crumbling sanity, your crushed dreams and broken soul. The old world, the safe world, is gone. You live in a savage land, a land without pity, without mercy. And it will eat you alive if you let it!

Some survivors will no doubt develop a strong belief system rooted in the principles of "terror management." Terror management is the conflict between the desire to live and knowing you are going to die. So you invent things to reassure yourself life has meaning, anything to nourish your self-esteem in the face of the cold, hard truth. A belief in immortality, in superiority of the human species, superiority of self, of country, or other things that keep you from giving up, from shutting down and going mad.

What does the apocalypse mean? How did it happen? Why did it happen now, to us? Reasons must be found, or if not found, made up to justify what we need to do to survive.

Look for most people to be paranoid and amoral compared to their pre-apocalypse selves. They may not *want* to behave this way, but experience has shown them not to let their guard down. That's how they lost friends and family. Given enough exposure through positive actions, not just words, these people can learn to trust again, but you must earn their loyalty.

## HERO AND VILLAIN PSYCHOLOGY

We've talked a lot about plots in a previous chapter, but what about character development? After all, fans may come to your story for the zombies, but they *stay* for the people. That's the reason *The Walking Dead* TV series has lasted as many seasons as it has. The zombies are great, you can't do it without them, but it's the human characters—their relationships and drama—that make it successful.

Study *The Walking Dead*. Study *Dawn of the Dead* (the 1978 original). They have great zombie action and great characters. And how do they do that? With great writing. You need to find similar ways for your characters to amuse, interest, or be liked by your readers. And don't forget to make them "love to hate" your human villains.

One way to get readers to like a character is to have him do something heroic or self-sacrificing when we first meet him. This is called a "save the cat" moment (or, if you prefer, "pet the dog," but don't take either term literally). Providing this moment of instant likability shows readers your character is a good person worth spending time with. But he should also be a flawed person, with one or two serious issues to work on, and these flaws should also be visible from the start. Whether or not the character overcomes his flaws or is consumed by them determines whether your story will have a "happy" or tragic ending. This inner growth (or failure to grow) is called character arc. Every major character should have one to some degree, but the main character should have the most.

Similarly, the villain should have a "kick the cat" moment when first revealed that proves just how ruthless and nasty he is. This display can be as obvious or subtle as you want (but not so subtle it slips past your readers). Do not make your villain a generic mustache-twirling maniac. Make him a badass, but a conflicted one. Let him be human, and morally complicated, but not pure evil. He has to have a few redeeming qualities that allow him to lead or at least briefly get along with what is left of society.

You pull this off by having him crack a joke or showing unexpected mercy—*even love*—then, when his humor or kindness blow up in his face, have him shrug and say something like, "See? That's why nice guys finish last."

That's the lesson he's learned. That's what twisted him into a villain, and that's what's going to get him killed in the end—but not before he's hurt a lot of people. Because nice guys really do finish last. The apocalypse hasn't changed that—in fact, it's made it more clear than ever. But you can't just be a horrible sadistic bastard to everyone either. That only works until you run into someone stronger than you—and chances are, your villainous power trip is going to create that enemy. Probably a whole lot of them.

## HERO AND VILLAIN CHARACTER ARCS

Heroes and villains lead by example. The fine line that separates them is in knowing their power and using it responsibly. Knowing when to apply force and how much. Knowing when diplomacy will serve you better. Making friends, forging allies. The art of compromise and sacrifice to keep things fair. All while staying in control. It's not easy. Most people screw it up one way or another. And while the pre-apocalypse world can forgive that, the post-apocalyptic world won't. Make too many small mistakes or just one big one, and you're dead. Your group is dead.

The real difference between the hero and villain is in their character arc. The hero struggles to grow (even if he fails) while the villain resists change at any cost. The villain fears change. He fears growth.

He doesn't think he needs it and tries to deprive everyone else of theirs.

For example, in the *Max Max* series, both the hockey- masked Lord Humungus from *The Road Warrior* (1981) and Immortan Joe from *Fury Road* (2015) believe might makes right. Why shouldn't they? They're on top of the food chain. They are not willing to share power or admit weakness because they rule by fear. They believe that any display of kindness or mercy will get them dead and their army dead. And so they kill, corrupt, or enslave everyone in their path to prove they are the mightiest power in the land.

This strategy works until they mess with the wrong guy, inadvertently turning a random loner into a deadly enemy that encourages others to rise up and rebel. But what if the Humungus or Immortan Joe had been more reasonable? What if they had been less interested in crushing Max than converting him into an ally? Or at least buying him off and honoring the deal? Max didn't want to fight. He just wanted to be left alone. By applying a military solution to what was essentially a diplomatic problem, these villains killed themselves and their armies. For what? To prove a point?

Compare these two ego-driven male villains to Tina Turner's Aunty Entity, the villain from *Max Max 3: Beyond Thunderdome* (1985). She uses diplomacy to trick Max into working for her and then tries to kill him when he backs out of the deal. When this strategy proves costly, Aunty realizes that rather than pursue Max, she could be home consolidating her power. She can safely end their feud because Max could care less about interfering with her empire, so where is the profit in killing an enemy she has grown to respect?

Because Aunty learns the lesson that Lord Humungus and Immortan Joe failed to learn, she gets to walk away at the end of the film with pride and power intact. Max also gets to walk away, which is all he really wanted to do in the first place. Whether or not Aunty will use this experience to become a better person or not is debatable.

Ending your story with a win/win for the hero and villain (or lose/lose, depending on your point of view) is rare and unlikely to satisfy everyone, but it is an interesting option, particularly if you want to bring the villain back in a sequel—perhaps this time as an ally against an even worse villain.

The villain is more important to the success of your story than the hero because he drives the action. And he does that because he believes he is the *hero* of *his* story. Treat him that way. Everything he says and does should be written with this goal in mind. He wants to look good, feel powerful, and get the last word in. He wants to win because that assures him he doesn't need to change when he is the character who needs change most.

The villain also represents the hero's dark side. He is what the hero will become should he fail to fix his flaws. That is why bad guys in movies tell the hero, "We're not so different, you and I." When the hero rejects these words (as they so often do), he fights and fails until he learns to accept that awful truth, and to work to change himself so he does not end up like the villain. That moment of self-awareness may come to the hero in minutes or years, depending on how you long you want his self-discovery to play out.

As soon as the hero realizes the villain is right, and determines to correct it, that is the moment the hero starts to win. And he will stay on the winning path.

The villain's true power over the hero is in holding him back, twisting him with hate, with fear, with doubt and self-loathing—all the things the villain secretly feels. Once those tricks no longer work, the villain is powerless. All his guns and goons don't matter. Even if the villain kills the hero, the hero wins a moral victory because he has proven himself the bigger man, the better man. And when the villain knows that, he will be crushed by it and carry that defeat forever.

For more advice on how to write heroes, villains, and everyone else (including groups or teams), read my bestseller, *Writing Heroes and Villains* (2018).

# 3

## HUMAN VILLAINS

IT'S NOT ENOUGH to have zombies, mutants, aliens, or killer robots. You need a human villain! Someone who can threaten, tempt, and strategize to make the post-apocalyptic world even worse for your characters. In this chapter, we're going to take a quick look at the six most common types of villains in the apocalypse:

- Cult
- Government Agency/Rogue Military
- Maniac
- Paramilitary Group/Biker Gang
- Traitor
- Tyrant

## CULT

Cults can take many forms, being either open to recruiting or closed. Closed groups may be restricted to extended family, members of the same religion or geographic area, etc. Cannibals and religious nuts are typical examples, such as The Termites and Wolves from *The Walking Dead*.

## GOVERNMENT AGENCY/ROGUE MILITARY

A sinister government agency or rogue military command present similar threats. They may take the shape of a "friendly" Governor-like enclave or a Negan-like private army that offer protection in return for whatever they want. They may claim they are operating under "government orders" and cite that as why the characters should obey.

If the agency is scientific in nature, experiments (such as for a vaccine) will be ruthlessly conducted without regard for law, rights, or dignity. The scientists in charge will be protected and enabled by soldiers. This creates a natural opportunity for the characters to exploit any schisms between the scientific and military factions.

## MANIAC

Maniacs are lone wolves driven by delusion. They are serial killers, spree killers, killers of opportunity. They may appear charming, but that charm wears thin as the monster within begins to surface, manifesting in a thousand different ways. Maniacs with the most charm become tyrants; those with less (or none at all), remain solo, or limit themselves to small groups.

The group may tolerate them for their lethal skills as long as they are directed against the group's enemies, but the best bond is one of family. In *Fear the Walking Dead*, Troy Otto is a maniac protected and enabled by his otherwise normal survivalist family. But if you want, the whole family can be insane, such as the cannibal Sawyers from *The Texas Chainsaw Massacre* (1974).

Those who fail to fit into even a small group of (relatively) normal people go it alone or partner up with another maniac, such as the two killers who teamed up to become *The Hillside Strangler* (2004).

Maniacs never think of themselves as crazy, and many believe they have some sort of special or divine purpose. That could be "sending pure souls to heaven" by killing them, purposely infecting survivors with the zombie virus as punishment "for their sins," or anything that justifies the terrible things they do.

For more about maniacs, including different types such as canni-bals, read my book, *Writing Monsters & Maniacs*. It features a handy list of questions to create a complete psychological profile of your maniac.

## PARAMILITARY/BIKER GANG

Paramilitary groups may be a mix of enclave and army: friendly to those like them, hostile to those who aren't. Biker gangs would behave the same, but be much more mobile. For examples of biker gangs, watch *Dawn of the Dead* (1978), *Raiders of Atlantis* (1983, aka *Atlantis Interceptors*), and *Sons of Anarchy* (TV, 2008-2014).

## TRAITOR

The traitor is another key villain type. He appears to be part of the group, but only cares about himself and his own selfish interests. He will honestly believe his way is the right way and he deserves to be in charge, not the current leader.

In *The Walking Dead*, Shane is a prime example of a traitor. In *Night of the Living Dead* (1968), it's Mr. Cooper. In *Day of the Dead* (1985), it's Captain Rhodes. While Cooper and Rhodes are selfish jerks likely to get everyone killed, Shane is that rare type of traitor who does actu-ally know what's best for his group. The problem is, he's terrible at convincing others he's right; his selfish desires (coveting his best friend's wife) and ruthless tactics repel the rest of the group and cause the majority to turn on him. It's ironic that it is only after his death that his way is proven right.

Traitors must have clear and specific motivations for why they are the way they are. We must see the seed of their hate happen, must watch the traitor nurse it until it blooms into a full-on power grab. A traitor in the starting group of characters can be conflicted, but cannot be an active, intentional traitor until circumstances push them to it. The exception is new survivors; when they show up, these can be or include traitors already. They may have a stronger allegiance to their own small group or to a larger group to which they secretly belong.

## TYRANT

In *The Walking Dead*, tyrants are exemplified by Negan and The Governor. Both rule very different kinds of paramilitary groups that were created after the apocalypse. Both are complicated men who present a charming exterior to hide their true evil.

The Governor further disguises his twisted ambition by saying it is for the common good, for law and order, to rebuild society and restore normalcy (under his iron hand, of course). This allows him to appear benevolent and easily recruit the best and brightest to his side. The Governor's people believe in him and his vision (at least the part he shares with them). They fight out of loyalty for a cause they think is worth dying for.

If the Governor is killed, his people will likely unite under a new leader. Whether that leader is better or worse than the Governor is up to you.

Negan, on the other hand, makes no attempt to disguise what he is: a thief, an extortionist, a murderous psychopath, and a powerful force for chaos and fear. This attracts the worst of the worst to his cause—the desperate, the broken, the criminal. Together, his gang ("The Saviors") become the ultimate post-apocalyptic protection racket. The Saviors fight out of fear of punishment, out of greed, lust, and revenge. Few, if any, will be loyal for any other reason. As long as Negan gets results that benefit his criminal followers, his position is secure. However, once he suffers one defeat too many, he will be challenged by his underlings, each eager to take his place.

That means if Negan is killed, he will almost always be replaced by a villain just as bad or even worse. However, unless the new leader has the same cult-like ability to hold the gang together, they will likely splinter and fall apart at some point.

# 4

## KILLER MACHINES

IT'S HARD NOT TO THINK of post-apocalyptic movies without thinking of killer machines from drones to *The Terminator* scouring the planet free of its human "infection." Other ideas include survivors adapting to new and unforgiving environments through technology, either as androids or cyborgs: *Robocop*, *The Six Million Dollar Man*, etc. Even zombies have been turned into cyborgs in films like *Return of the Living Dead 3*.

### ANDROIDS

Androids are robots with a human-like appearance. They may be virtually indistinguishable from humans or built with one or more characteristics that identify them as robots. Androids are equipped with artificial intelligence and programmed to act in ways similar to humans. Due to their human-like appearance and behavior, androids make ideal companions, assassins, and spies.

Depending on their programming, androids may, over time, become obsessed with learning how to become more human (if treated well) or less human (if treated badly). The complicated web of human emotions are the primary stumbling block for androids. They are programmed to mimic emotions, but cannot actually *feel* them. The quest to truly feel and understand emotions is what drive many androids' character arcs.

Another option is for humans to insert themselves into android bodies, either temporarily, or permanently, perhaps as a way to live forever or survive in the post-apocalyptic world. What kind of android body and attributes would you want if you could remake yourself from scratch? The sky's the limit, or at least your bank account. Check out *Surrogates* (2009) for more on that.

## SAMPLE ANDROIDS

- *Westworld* (1973 and 2016-present TV remake)
- *The Stepford Wives* (1975)
- *Alien* (1979)
- *Android* (1982)
- *Halloween III: Season of the Witch* (1982)
- *The Terminator* (1984)
- *Blade Runner* (1982)
- *Aliens* (1986)
- *Star Trek: The Next Generation* (TV, 1987-1992)
- *Terminator 2: Judgment Day* (1991)
- *Screamers* (1995)
- *A.I. Artificial Intelligence* (2001)
- *Imposter* (2001)
- *Surrogates* (2009)
- *Ex Machina* (2014)
- *Chappie* (2015)
- *Humans* (TV, 2015-present)
- *Blade Runner 2049* (2017)

## CYBORGS

A cyborg is a human or other creature whose physical abilities have been enhanced beyond its natural limits by artificial replacements or modifications. These cybernetic parts may or may not be noticeable; they could be covered with synthetic skin, for example. In humans, the more organic parts that are replaced, the more anger, depression, and mental illness the cyborg may have, as he feels "more machine than man." *Robocop* (1987), dealt with this struggle.

The cyborg theme is one of self-acceptance and identity: If you're not who you were, who are you now? Man? Machine? Something more? Something less?

How are cyborgs treated in your story world? Are they primarily wounded veterans and accident victims, or do people seek out such procedures? Why? Is this for a job, military service, a fetish, or personal fulfillment?

## CYBERPUNK CYBORGS

When you think of cyborgs, you may see a picture of someone who is half-man and half-machine, but there is another type of cyborg popularized in cyberpunk films and fiction like *Johnny Mnemonic* (1995). These cyborgs have cybernetic implants in their skulls—data ports they can use to download memories, information, languages, or specialized skills as a shortcut to traditional forms of learning. What if you could instantly become a master of anything you want? Think of the potential for education, careers, and espionage!

## CYBORGS EXIST NOW

Cyborgs do not belong solely to the realm of science fiction. People with electronic artificial limbs are the most noticeable, but technically, any wearable or implanted electronic or prosthetic device is cybernetic; this includes pacemakers, hearing aids, and contact lenses.

What would happen if a mad scientist or enterprising criminal could hijack these devices?

For example, sending subliminal suggestions through a hearing aid to brainwash a victim? Or blackmailing a man to commit a crime for him or else his pacemaker will be turned off? Or remote controlling a man's cybernetic arm to strangle someone to death? The possibilities are endless!

## CYBORG VULNERABILTY

Cyborgs are vulnerable to EMP (electro-magnetic pulse) effects that can cause unshielded implants to go dead. Depending on what these implants control, this can be a mere nuisance or absolutely crippling.

## SAMPLE CYBORGS

There are plenty of cyborgs to be inspired by, from Darth Vader to the Borg to the Daleks and Cybermen of *Dr. Who*:

- *Dr. Who and the Daleks* (1965)
- *Daleks' Invasion Earth 2150 A.D.* (1966)
- *Star Wars* (1977)
- *The Six Million Dollar Man* (TV, 1974-78)
- *The Bionic Woman* (TV, 1976-78)
- *Robocop* (1987)
- *Cyborg* (1989)
- *Tetsuo, the Iron Man* (1989)
- *Return of the Living Dead 3* (1993)
- *Ghost in the Shell* (1995 anime and 2017 live-action remake)
- *Johnny Mnemonic* (1995)
- *Star Trek: First Contact* (1996)
- *Teen Titans* (TV, 2003-06)
- *Iron Man* (2008)
- *Captain America: The Winter Soldier* (2014)
- *Upgrade* (2018)

## ROBOTS

Robots are autonomous or semi-autonomous machines programmed to carry out complex actions. They may or may not have a human- or animal-like appearance, and may be any size, mobile or stationary. Robots can be used in hazardous situations and hostile environments without endangering human life. They can also maximize production efficiency in factories.

Replacing humans, while having obvious benefits, breeds anger and anti-robot sentiment in the humans who were replaced. Many humans fear not only job loss to robots, but what happens if robots become sentient and decide to exterminate humanity.

The ethical use of robots and what governs their behavior is also in question. Can robots achieve self-awareness through artificial intelligence, and if they can, are they entitled to the same rights exercised by humans? If not, aren't they our slaves? And what if the robots refuse to accept our decision? What if they choose to enslave or destroy us?

There are many examples of military, industrial, and commercial robots in use or being developed today, from drones to vacuum cleaners to self-driving vehicles and space probes.

## NANOBOTS

Nanobots are a new type of robot to watch out for. They are bacteria-sized robots that can be injected into people to perform surgery or into machines to repair them, but they can also be used as weapons. They could assassinate enemies, cripple computer systems, and wreak all kinds of havoc. Some speculate nanobots could cover the earth, devouring everything and turning the planet into "gray goo."

## SAMPLE ROBOTS

Need more inspiration? Check out these famous robots:

- *The Phantom Creeps* (1939)
- *Gog* (1954)
- *Forbidden Planet* (1956)
- *Kronos* (1957)
- *Lost in Space* (TV, 1965-1968)
- *Demon Seed* (1977)
- *Star Wars* (1977)
- *Battlestar Galactica* (TV, 1978-79)
- *The Black Hole* (1979)
- *The Shape of Things to Come* (1979)
- *Saturn 3* (1980)
- *The Transformers* (TV, 1984-1987)
- *Voltron, Defender of the Universe* (TV, 1984-85)
- *Robotech* (TV, 1985)
- *Chopping Mall* (1986)
- *Short Circuit* (1986)
- *Robocop* (1987)
- *Robot Jox* (1989)
- *Hardware* (1990)
- *The Iron Giant* (1999)
- *Pacific Rim* (2013)
- *Robot Overlords* (2014)
- *Rogue One* (2016)
- *Solo* (2018)

# 5

## MUTANTS AND ANIMALS

MUTANTS ARE NATURALLY OCCURRING or the product of scientific experimentation or exposure to radiation, chemicals, or other unusual substances. Depending on the mutation, mutants represent an evolutionary leap forward or backward.

Think about the environment of your post-apocalyptic story world. Has there been a dramatic change that demands species adapt or die? Have mutagenic chemicals or radiation been released? What effect are they having? Is it a slow change, or sudden? In *Damnation Alley* (1977), within a few years of nuclear war, scorpions grow as large as dogs and cockroaches scour cities in swarms, feeding on human flesh.

### MUTANTS MAKING MUTANTS

Another idea is mutant parasites that enter a host organism, changing it from within. The David Cronenberg "body horror" film, *Shivers* (1975) features a parasite that stimulates its host's sexual impulses. Unfortunately, the parasite *overstimulates* the host, turning them into violent, sex-crazed zombies.

It doesn't have to be parasites that transform people or wildlife, it could be a virus or toxic waste. In *Mutants* (2009), the virus acts like it does in a zombie movie, and those it infects mutate into subhuman cannibals. In *C.H.U.D.* and *Mutant* (both 1984), exposure to toxic waste turns people into cannibalistic monsters.

## SUPERHEROES AND SUPERVILLAINS

Mutants have long been popular as heroes and villains in comic books. People long for extraordinary powers, and depending on what kind of person they are, they could use those powers for good, evil, or selfish reasons.

The most realistic depiction of what would happen when people gain super powers can be seen in *Chronicle* (2012). An example of an entire post-apocalyptic world reformed into a feudal superhero dystopia is the bestselling *Red Queen* series by Victoria Aveyard.

The source of your story's superpowers could be aliens, government experiments, radiation, whatever you can imagine.

## ANIMALS

Animals could be affected by radiation, gene splicing, or any number of strange phenomena, turning on man and bringing their own kind of apocalypse. This can be seen in films like Alfred Hitchcock's *The Birds* (1963), *Chosen Survivors* (1974), and *Kingdom of the Spiders* (1977).

To make things even more apocalyptic, you could give the animals diseases like rabies or bubonic plague, or maybe the virus affects humans differently, turning them into zombies or devolving them into a primitive state, perhaps as subhuman caveman cannibals!

## HOW TO WRITE MUTANTS AND ANIMALS

When your villain is not human or human-like, you have your work cut out for you. But all is not lost! Many successful books feature non-human point of view chapters, such as the mutant, man-eating rats in the opening to James Herbert's post-apocalyptic novel, *Domain*:

*They scurried through the darkness, shadowy creatures living in permanent night.*

*They had learned to become still, to be the darkness, when the huge monsters roared above and filled the tunnels with thunder, assaulting the black refuge—their cold, damp sanctuary—with rushing lights and deadly crushing weight. They would cower as the ground beneath them shook, the walls around them trembled; and they would wait until the rushing thing had passed, not afraid but necessarily wary, for it was an inveterate invader but one which killed the careless.*

*They had learned to keep within the confines of their underworld, to venture out only when their own comforting darkness was sistered with the darkness above. For they had a distant race-memory of an enemy, a being whose purpose was to destroy them.*

— JAMES HERBERT, DOMAIN

There's more, of course. This is the third book in Herbert's immensely popular *Rats Trilogy,* and the author has to finish setting up that these are mutant rats, that the bombs have dropped, and the world is now a very different place. A place where the tables have turned, and man, the rats' most hated enemy, is now easy prey in the ruins of post-apocalyptic London.

## SAMPLE MUTANTS AND ANIMALS

- *Freaks* (1932)
- *The Island of Lost Souls* (1932)
- *Godzilla* (1954)
- *Them!* (1954)
- *This Island Earth* (1955)
- *Tarantula!* (1955)
- *The Amazing Colossal Man* (1957)
- *Attack of the Crab Monsters* (1957)
- *The Incredible Shrinking Man* (1957)

- *Attack of the 50 Foot Woman* (1958)
- *The Fly* (1958 and 1986 remake)
- *The Alligator People* (1959)
- *The Flesh Eaters* (1964)
- *The Deadly Bees* (1966)
- *Octaman* (1971)
- *Frogs* (1972)
- *The Twilight People* (1972)
- *Invasion of the Bee Girls* (1973)
- *Sssssss* (1973)
- *Chosen Survivors* (1974)
- *The Mutations* (1974)
- *Bug* (1975)
- *Shivers* (1975, aka *They Came from Within*)
- *The Food of the Gods* (1976)
- *Squirm* (1976)
- *Ants* (1977)
- *Damnation Alley* (1977)
- *Day of the Animals* (1977)
- *Empire of the Ants* (1977)
- *The Island of Dr. Moreau* (1977 and 1996 remake)
- *Kingdom of the Spiders* (1977)
- *The Man from Atlantis* (TV, 1977-78)
- *The Incredible Hulk* (TV, 1978-82)
- *Piranha* (1978)
- *Spawn of the Slithis* (1978)
- *The Swarm* (1978)
- *Terror Out of the Sky* (TV, 1978)
- *The Brood* (1979)
- *Nightwing* (1979)
- *Alligator* (1980)
- *Humanoids from the Deep* (1980)
- *The Funhouse* (1981)
- *Piranha Part 2: The Spawning* (1981)
- *Basket Case* (1982)

- *Deadly Eyes* (1982)
- *C.H.U.D.* (1984)
- *Mutant* (1984)
- *The Toxic Avenger* (1985)
- *Hell Comes to Frogtown (1988)*
- *The Fly 2* (1989)
- *Total Recall* (1990)
- *Outbreak* (1995)
- *Mimic* (1997)
- *Bats* (1999)
- *Deep Blue Sea* (1999)
- *X-Men* (2000)
- *Spider-Man* (2002)
- *The Cave* (2005)
- *The Hills Have Eyes* series (2006-07)
- *Wrong Turn* series (2006-14)
- *Splinter* (2008)
- *Mutants* (2009)
- *Splice* (2009)
- *Captain America: The First Avenger* (2011)
- *Chronicle* (2012)
- *Deadpool* (2016)
- *Logan* (2017)
- *Deadpool 2* (2018)

If you're looking for help writing or describing aliens, pick up my *Science Fiction Writers' Phrase Book* and *Writing Monsters and Maniacs*.

# 6

## ZOMBIE ANIMALS

IN MOST ZOMBIE APOCALYPSE SCENARIOS, animals are immune to the virus. In this case, you must decide if zombies do not see animals as food or if they will still target and eat them. Regardless, zombies will respond to animal noise, movement, and attacks.

The zombies in the George A. Romero universe (*Night of the Living Dead, Dawn of the Dead*, etc.) do not feed on animals, although in *NotLD*, we do see a zombie eat a bug.

In Robert Kirkman's *The Walking Dead*, zombies eagerly eat animals and are apparently unable to distinguish between them and people; that is, they do not seem to prefer one over the other. However, the zombie virus cannot jump species; there are no zombie animals in Romero's or Kirkman's world.

This is not the case in the *Resident Evil* franchise, which famously features zombie dogs and other animals. In the SyFy Channel film, *Zombie Apocalypse* (2012), we even see a zombie tiger!

Whether you want to complicate your apocalypse with zombie animals is up to you. However, you should know most purists *hate* the idea. Not only can it be laughable (imagine being chased by Paris Hilton and her army of little yappy zombie purse dogs), but it ruins two important elements of the zombie apocalypse fantasy:

1. The ability to survive by hunting or domesticating animals becomes much more difficult; and
2. It disproves the classic theory that the virus is nature's way of restoring the planet to its pre-human condition. If the animal population fails to survive, then undoing man's environmental damage won't matter.

## ZOMBIES BEFRIENDING ANIMALS

On a related note, if zombies can learn or remember skills in your story, then it may be possible, if not probable, for them to use animals —not necessarily as food, but as partners.

In *Tombs of the Blind Dead* (1972), zombified Knights Templar ride undead horses, and in *Survival of the Dead* (2009), we see a modern zombie riding a horse. In both films, the zombies had a strong pre-existing bond with their animals before death.

Another idea could be for a zombie veterinarian, pet shop owner, pet lover, or zookeeper to continue to care for her animals after she reanimates. Most likely, she would continue to "feed" dead animals with the flesh of her victims.

# 7

# INFECTED CHARACTERS

WHEN A CHARACTER IS EXPOSED to the zombie virus (or any similar plague-like virus), you have to decide whether they become infected or not. There are no hard and fast "rules" for how the infection spreads. It's up to you to choose how people turn into zombies, mutants, or whatever. Here are the most popular options for zombies:

1. Everyone is infected. The virus lies dormant until the host dies from *any* cause. Being bitten injects enough new virus cells to activate the dormant ones, telling them to accelerate and kill the host. This is the original way popularized in *Night of the Living Dead* (1968). It's also the most popular method.

2. Only people who are bitten or scratched can turn; *Dawn of the Dead* (2004 remake) used this method. Be aware that choosing this will slow the spread of the virus unless you make your zombies fast instead of the classic slow variety.

3. In addition to bites, zombies have a breath weapon (projectile vomiting infected blood) which they use to infect people at a short distance—about five to ten feet, max (counting particulates in the air), depending on how

"extreme" you want to be. Note that zombies, like people, have a limited amount of blood in their system, so they can't vomit more than a few times, and each time they do, their range will decrease. Only people bitten, scratched (or blasted in the face with vomit) become zombies. This method was used in *28 Days Later* (2002) and *Dead Men Walking* (2005).

If you want something besides a virus to create your zombies, then you'll have to put some thought into what that is and how it works. Such changes don't need to be drastic and can more or less conform to one of the above methods.

For example, in *The Girl with All the Gifts* (Novel, 2014, and film, 2016), the "hungries" are humans controlled by a mutant fungus similar to Ophiocordyceps unilateralis, the species that creates "zombie ants" in the real world. Only people who get bitten turn into hungries. So it's pretty much "the same, but different." That's what Hollywood and your readers want: a twist. There's no need to reinvent the wheel, just slap a new rim on it and hit the gas.

## ✓ TRANSMISSION BY BITE

Bites are the primary way the zombie virus spreads. To transmit the virus, the bite must puncture the skin, mixing the zombie's saliva with the blood of its victim.

## ✓ TRANSMISSION BY SCRATCH

Scratches from zombie fingernails may or may not cause infection; it depends on how recently the zombie has touched infected material (including its own saliva during feeding). Scratches are more likely to transmit any secondary diseases the zombie is carrying, rather than the zombie virus itself (see below).

## ✓ TRANSMISSION BY BODILY FLUIDS

Unless the zombie's fluids get into a character's eyes, nose, mouth, ears (or other orifices), infection from anything other than a bite is not automatic. Obviously, having unprotected sexual intercourse with a zombie is a bad idea for this and many other reasons. Fortunately, zombies don't breathe or sneeze, so they can't transmit airborne pathogens the way humans do.

## ✓ TRANSMISSION BY CONTAMINATED WATER

Zombies floating in or moving through water will contaminate it with both the zombie virus and any other diseases they carry, so boiling or purifying water before drinking is a must. Contaminated wells or water pumps were used as plot devices in both *The Walking Dead* and *Z Nation*.

## HOW THE VIRUS WORKS

Without getting too technical, the zombie virus attacks the central nervous system, shutting down the host's organs and brain. You can make this as fast or slow as you like. It can be subtle or disgusting, such as the host bleeding out every orifice like they would from a hemorrhagic fever. For examples, look to Ebola and Marburg in the real world; these and other filoviruses were chronicled in Richard Preston's nonfiction shocker, *The Hot Zone* (1995). A fictional example is the Motaba virus in *Outbreak* (1995).

Once the host is dead, the virus works on completing its takeover of the host's body and brain functions. Again, this can be as fast or slow as you like. Once the process is complete, the virus reanimates the corpse as a zombie. Zombies exist for one purpose: to spread the virus. They do this by biting victims. Eating them is unnecessary (and even counterproductive), but my theory is the consumption of human flesh is caused by one of the following:

1. The virus isn't sure it's successfully passed itself on through a single bite, so it keeps attacking until it's absolutely sure of infecting the new host, perhaps by receiving a return signal of some kind from its transplanted cells; and/or
2. The zombie may insist on eating or taking multiple bites because it is a half-remembered, pleasurable activity. The virus either does not notice or does care, or else it is powerless to interfere with the zombie taking this action.

Newly reanimated zombies will typically be slower and more awkward than normal as they adjust to their undead state. They may also be less aggressive and even recognize people, objects, and places from their life. This "recognition" is partial and confused, but may be enough to temporarily redirect them from attacking a loved one if another target is present. It may motivate the new zombie to remain in some place that had great meaning to them. Or they might leave, but take a beloved object with them.

In *Night of the Living Dead* (the 1990 remake), we see a female zombie holding a baby doll; this presumably represents the infant daughter she may have eaten and replaced with the toy. In *Dawn of the Dead* (1978), a "gun nut" zombie is fascinated by rifles and can be distracted from attacking by handing him one; this happens twice in the film. The poor zombie never does figure out how to fire it.

Not so in the sequel, *Day of the Dead* (1985). In that film, after being "civilized" by a mad scientist, "Bub," a former military veteran, not only remembers how to shoot, he can actually hit a target! Also in that film, we hear stories of zombies driving cars and doing other half-remembered activities from their human lives—all with disastrous effect. And in *Land of the Dead* (2005), we see a whole town full of zombies going through the motions of their old lives, from a gas station attendant to an entire brass band.

## INCUBATION TIME

The incubation time for the zombie virus is one to six hours, with three being average (feel free to change this to fit your story). The more wounded a victim is, the faster the infection sets in. This may be due to having had more of the virus introduced into the body, or simply because a severely wounded subject is less able to resist the effects.

Within three to six hours of infection, symptoms begin to appear: fever, nausea, joint pain and swelling. These vary in both severity and onset by the overall health of the subject. They will not appear all at once but sneak up gradually. According to *Dawn of the Dead* (1978) and most zombie lore, no one has ever lived longer than three days after infection.

Infected people should be considered immediately contagious and reasonable precautions taken when handling them, especially near any bite areas. The virus could potentially seep out through their pores when they sweat, through their tears when they cry, when they kiss you, etc. However, to the best of my knowledge, no one in any zombie material I've seen has passed the virus on in this way. That doesn't mean they can't do it in your zombie story. It might be a nasty twist that makes saying goodbye even harder for people who can't even hug or kiss their loved ones goodbye. Yet another part of their life the virus has stolen from them.

## WHAT TO DO WITH THE INFECTED

Most people will try to help the infected individual, even when they know there is nothing they can do but keep them company and make their last moments comfortable. Other more pragmatic (or ruthless) individuals will argue for killing the infected outright, "before they have a chance to turn." Or they will insist on abandoning them, perhaps with a gun and one bullet so the infected can die on their own terms without fear of coming back as an undead monster.

The disagreement between those who want to do what they can

for the infected—not what is best for the group—and those who don't want to share the same shelter with them is a powerful scene. Be sure to play it out with plenty of raw emotion. These types of disputes are ripe for creating rival factions to form within a group. It's also a chance for the group to split up.

## PROGRESSION OF SYMPTOMS

The following timeline assumes a non-lethal bite where the bleeding is stopped and first aid applied. Feel free to use or modify this schedule as needed.

Immediately After Infection: If the bitten area is amputated quickly, this might be enough to prevent the virus from invading the rest of the body. We see this tactic save a life in both *Day of the Dead* (1985) and *The Walking Dead*, Season 3, Episode 1, "Seed." Obviously, this only works with arms and legs.

- **Day 1 (1-6 Hours After Being Infected):** The bite area is swollen, red, and infected. The infection may or may not appear to be briefly slowed by antibiotics and proper wound hygiene, but ultimately, these tactics are insufficient to stop the infection from spreading and killing the host. Subject begins to experience a slight fever and the beginning of a headache as well as joint pain. They may also suffer mild dissociation, broken sleep, and nightmares.
- **Day 2 (Morning):** Wake with a splitting headache. Fever worsens; the infected feels like they are "burning up." Cold sweat. Become restless. Thoughts disordered, sometimes sad, sometimes angry. Bite area worsens and infection spreads in all directions.
- **Day 2 (Afternoon):** Fever breaks. Individual is cold, clammy. Can't get warm. Headache has dulled now, but brain feels numb. Subject is lethargic, depressed, has difficulty thinking or staying focused on a task or subject. Needs to sleep but still suffers nightmares. Infection now

covers most of their body. Everything hurts. Weaker individuals may slip into a coma at this point; stronger ones can hold on and remain lucid, but not much longer.

- **Day 2 (Evening):** Most subjects slip into a coma at this point and die quietly some hours later. Stronger ones may fade in and out of consciousness before dying. A "lucky" few resist the coma and even make it to the next day.

- **Day 3 (Variable):** If the subject wakes up, they are barely able to move or function. Their thoughts are hazy, hallucinations rampant. Some may insist on getting up to accomplish one last task or grand gesture, though they are probably incapable of following through. Body temperature is the lowest possible. Everything is numb. Organs are shutting down. Senses grow dim and confused. It feels like all their thoughts are in slow motion. At some point, they simply can't go on. They slip into a coma and die.

- **After Death (Variable):** The virus assumes control and reanimates the corpse as a zombie. In some movies, this happens in seconds, in others minutes, and for some, hours. Rather than a one size fits all reanimation timetable, you can vary it by the individual, based on whatever criteria you want. In other words, you let the needs of the story dictate who turns when. However, you need to be careful with this. If the reanimation times are wildly inconsistent, it will seriously hurt your story's credibility.

## ZOMBIES AS CARRIERS OF OTHER DISEASES

The primary method of transmission for other diseases zombies carry comes from being in close contact with them or areas covered in whatever mess they leave behind.

As walking piles of decay that tend to be covered in the rotting flesh and blood of their victims, zombies may carry other types of communicable diseases: some deadly, some not. The worst include bubonic plague, cholera, smallpox, and typhus. Also, any creatures that feed on them (crows, flies, rats, vultures, worms, etc.) could spread the disease.

*The Walking Dead* examined this in Season Four, Episode 2, "Infected." In that episode, humans and zombies become infected with swine flu after eating sick wild boar. Swine flu is a zoonotic infection (one capable of spreading from species to species, in this case, from pigs to people—including zombies). The swine flu kills people (turning them into zombies) and also makes confronting "flu zombies" even more dangerous. That's because unlike the zombie virus, swine flu is airborne. Now it's not just the undead characters have to worry about, it's *any* contact with infected humans as well.

At least with bites, you can see who's infected and know who's going to turn; with flu, you can't know, at least not for several days. And there's no guarantee the infected are going to die. Abandoning or quarantining the sick until they recover or perish are the best methods to limit infection, but these can cause moral dilemmas as survivors argue over which option is right.

The incubation for regular flu is one to four days, with two being average. Infected people can be contagious from one day before symptoms manifest through five to seven afterward. With swine flu, those numbers change: the infected are contagious for one day before the first symptoms appear through a full week after. After exposure, swine flu takes an average of five days to kick in. Plenty of time for people to think they're in the clear and infect others.

In a hostile post-apocalyptic world without access to modern medicine and antibiotics, let alone proper nutrition or hydration, any infection can be serious.

✓ **Important Tip:** Fleas, ticks, and mosquitos do not feed on the dead and will *never* target zombies. However, they may feed on the blood of infected *living* humans and transmit the virus that way, similar to how they spread malaria or Lyme disease.

# 8

# ZOMBIE CHARACTERS

Zombies as full-fledged characters are rare. Most are walk-ons that barely warrant a line or two of description before getting their brains blown out. That's because unintelligent zombies aren't that interesting. What makes them work as villains is either the human (or intelligent zombie) commanding them, or that they exist as a force of nature to highlight the strengths and weaknesses of the human characters—the ones they are trying to convert into mindless undead.

One quick and easy way to inject a little personality into your undead is for the human characters to give them nicknames. These can be funny, rude, affectionate, etc. This usually only applies to zombies that aren't going to be immediately killed and likely to stick around for some reason (see *Dawn of the Dead*'s 2004 remake for an exception where characters give zombies the names of celebrities they resemble before shooting them). Zombies or types of zombies that deviate from their normal behavior are also likely to be named.

Example "pet" names for zombies: Assface, Barf-breath, Cyclops (missing an eye), Dr. Tongue (missing lower jaw so tongue hangs out), Eddie (inspired by Iron Maiden's mascot), Gollum, Pusbag, Stinky.

## INTELLIGENT ZOMBIES

In order to be a true point of view character, a zombie *must* have some semblance of sentience and emotion remaining to give the reader something to relate to. Ask yourself, "Why is this zombie special?"

- Was the zombie "civilized" by an authority figure or scientist as "Bub" was in *Day of the Dead* (1985)?
- Is the zombie controlled by an invention to "civilize" it, such as the shock collar in *Fido* (2006)?
- Does the zombie even know it's dead? Does it continue to more or less think and act like it's alive, finding excuses and rationalizations to justify its altered appetite as well as its mental and physical state? "New Years' Day," an episode of *Fear Itself* (TV, 2008) explores this, as well as my own short story, "Two Girls, A Guy, and the End of the World."
- Is the zombification process so slow or different that the zombie retains its intelligence and personality for an indefinite period as in *Return of the Living Dead* (1985) and *Return of the Living Dead 3* (1993)?
- Was the zombie the result of a scientific experiment like in *Monster Island* (Novel, 2004)?
- Did the zombie receive a vaccine with unexpected side effects like *Z Nation* (TV, 2014-present)?
- Is the zombie a mutant? How and why did the virus mutate? What makes this zombie different?

Intelligent zombies may be driven to interact with humans only as sources of food, amusement, or obsession (typically love or revenge). They may hate the living and lash out at them as a way to mourn their own lost humanity, or as a way to justify their superiority, or give meaning to their existence. However, they usually keep their interactions with the living to a minimum, both as a form of self-preservation and to limit any sense of loss from watching loved ones age and die while they go on forever.

Intelligent zombies having relationships with humans are usually restricted to romantic horror comedies: *My Boyfriend's Back* (1993), *Warm Bodies* (2013), *Burying the Ex* (2014), and *Life After Beth* (2014). However, there's no reason you can't explore a relationship that's more serious in tone, like *Return of the Living Dead 3* (1993).

## ZOMBIE GOALS AND MOTIVATIONS

As former humans, intelligent zombies have many of the same needs as the living: food, shelter, security. Where they differ is in the *nature* of that food. The zombie may have different needs for the kind and number of companionship it requires, as well as desire for a mate (that is, if it still has a sex drive and ability to perform).

What does the zombie character want beyond basic survival? To be left alone? To gain power? To fit in? To find a cure? A zombie that can control its appetite could be a valuable asset to a human group:

- The zombie could scout ahead and not be eaten.
- The zombie could spy on other humans who do not realize it is intelligent.
- The zombie could convince other zombies to attack a hostile location with supplies its friends need.
- The zombie is the perfect guard, never needing sleep.
- The zombie *might* be able to prevent or at least slow down an attack on its friends by other zombies.

How concerned about decomposition and the deterioration of its mental and physical abilities does the zombie character need to be? It is unlikely to feel pain or fatigue, which can be a blessing and a curse. If the zombie can't feel its injuries, it won't know it needs to stop or correct its course of action before damaging itself further.

If it's dead, how can the zombie heal? The answer is it probably can't, so it must bind and sew up its wounds and cosmetically hide its decay in some manner. Does it have a "human" disguise and how effective is it? Is it waterproof? Does it only disguise its visible skin?

How much makeup does it use and how much of a supply does it have? What happens when it can no longer disguise what it is?

## FRIENDLY ZOMBIES

Friendly zombies will initially be extremely loyal to any humans willing to take them in. They desire a return to normalcy, to companionship, to everything they used to have. Yet living with humans is hard. Not just suffering their suspicion and prejudice, but the zombie must control its own desire to eat their living friends and allies. A zombie that feels abused or mistreated may betray or attack the group, but only if no other option for relief presents itself.

## HOSTILE ZOMBIES

Hostile zombies are likely megalomaniacs, undead versions of *The Walking Dead*'s Governor or Negan. They may see themselves as the next stage of evolution. To protect themselves and enforce this belief, they will seek to raise a zombie army.

Hostile zombies who aren't megalomaniacs may instead be motivated by old feuds and twisted desires, but this is hate and revenge on an individual scale. They may employ other zombies as cover and helpers, but they have no grand ambition beyond satisfying their immediate goals.

## ZOMBIE CHARACTER RESOURCES

- For stories told entirely from a zombie's perspective, watch *Colin* (2008) and "New Years' Day," an episode of *Fear Itself* (TV, 2008).
- "Bub" in *Day of the Dead* (1985) and "Big Daddy" in *Land of the Dead* (2005) are examples of zombies evolving semi-sentience and retaining elements of their human personality and profession.

- For domesticated zombie servants, watch *Fido* (2006).
- More advanced but conditionally sentient zombies can be seen in *Warm Bodies* (2013) and *Freaks of Nature* (2015).
- For fully sentient zombies, watch *iZombie* (TV, 2015-present). Also read the novels *Monster Island* by David Wellington (2004) and *The Girl with All the Gifts* by M. R. Carey (2014, also a 2016 film).
- For half-human/half-zombies, watch the transformation of "Murphy" throughout the first three seasons of *Z Nation* (TV, 2014-present). Over time, he learns he can telepathically control zombies and mind control the people he bites, which also makes them immune to the zombie virus.

# 9

## TYPES OF ZOMBIES

MOST ZOMBIES ARE MINDLESS MONSTERS created from dead bodies. They come in five types, including those brought back to life by:

1. Demons
2. Psychic energy
3. Science
4. Viruses
5. Voodoo (or other magic)

Most are slaves ("hosts") to whatever force reanimated them.

A sixth type of zombie are not undead, but living infected; I call these zombies "virus maniacs." They are people or animals infected with a virus or other toxic substance (perhaps radiation) that does not kill them, but reduces them to a crazed, violent, often zombie-like state. These types of zombies can be seen in films like *28 Days Later, I Drink Your Blood, Night of the Comet,* and *Pontypool.* They can be found at the end of this chapter, lurking just on the edge of your sanity…

So which type of zombie is right for your apocalypse? That's up to you. Each presents a unique opportunity to put a fresh twist on the end of the world. Choose wisely, but feel free to tinker and tweak.

Who knows what you can come up with? Maybe you can combine two or more types of zombies into one, or mix and match different strengths and weaknesses. For example, *28 Days Later* made fast (but living) zombies, while the *Dawn of the Dead* remake took that idea and simply made its undead zombies fast. There's no reason you can't do something similar...

## DEMONIC ZOMBIES

Demonic zombies are reanimated corpses that blend cunning, cruelty, and super-strength. Some can teleport or transform their bodies into terrifying shapes. They may appear alive until they attack.

These zombies may or may not eat human flesh; their primary purpose is to torment, infect, and murder the living, with bonus points for damning the souls of their victims while creating another host body to possess. Those killed by them may or may not reanimate. Whether or not they do depends on the rules you create:

1. Is it a psychic or spiritual virus that requires victim consent to kill its host as in a traditional demonic possession movie? Then not every corpse reanimates, only those too weak to resist the demon's evil.
2. Is it a physical virus with a psychic or supernatural component that does *not* require victim consent? Then it will automatically kill its host, as in a traditional virus zombie movie.

The "Deadites" from Sam Raimi's *Evil Dead* films are a prime example of the first option, while the *[REC]* and *Quarantine* series zombies are examples of the second.

Note that with demonic zombies, sometimes most of the zombies aren't very smart and act like regular virus zombies, while the ringleader zombie (often in the body of a defrocked priest or warlock) has telepathic command over them. Both Lucio Fulci's *City of the Living Dead* (1980) and *The Beyond* (1981) deal with demonic ringleader zombies opening the "gates of hell" that allow the demonic dead to rise.

In *Messiah of Evil* (1973), demonic zombies are created by a spiritual virus, curse, or other unseen supernatural force. In Stephen King's *Pet Sematary* (1989), they are created by burying the dead in a cursed native burial ground; evil spirits (possibly related to the Wendigo) bring them back to life.

The last type of demonic zombie are the dried-out reanimated corpses of the devil-worshipping Knights Templar seen in *Tombs of the Blind Dead* (1972) and its three sequels. These undead knights are clad in robes and armor, wield swords, and rise from their graves to drink the blood of the living. Though they cannot speak, they can still think, and coordinate their attacks both on foot and horseback, riding skeletal war horses. They cannot see, hence their name ("The Blind Dead"), but rather rely on their keen sense of hearing to track victims.

The Blind Dead mix certain qualities of liches, mummies, revenants, skeletons, and vampires, so they are a bit hard to classify. I've included them here because they owe their unlife to a pact with the Devil.

## SAMPLE DEMONIC ZOMBIES

- *Tombs of the Blind Dead* (1972)
- *Messiah of Evil* (1973)
- *Return of the Blind Dead* (1973)
- *The Ghost Galleon* (1974, aka *Horror of the Zombies*)
- *Night of the Seagulls* (1975, aka *Night of the Death Cult*)
- *The Beyond* (1981)
- *The Evil Dead* (1981 and 2013 remake)
- *City of the Living Dead* (1983, aka *The Gates of Hell*)
- *Demons* (1985)
- *Demons 2* (1986)
- *Evil Dead 2* (1987)
- *Flesheater* (1988)

- *Night of the Demons* (1988 and 2009 remake)
- *Pet Sematary* (1989)
- *Army of Darkness* (1992)
- *Pet Sematary 2* (1992)
- *Night of the Demons 2* (1994)
- *Tales from the Crypt: Demon Knight* (1995)
- *Night of the Demons 3* (1997)
- *Versus* (2000)
- *[REC]* (2007)
- *Quarantine* (2008)
- *[REC] 2* (2009)
- *Quarantine 2* (2011)
- *JeruZalem* (2015)
- *Ash vs. Evil Dead* (TV, 2015-2018)

## PSYCHIC ZOMBIES

Psychic zombies are powered by a combination of telepathy and psychokinesis (aka telekinesis). A living psychic, a ghost, a demon, or some other energy being brings a corpse or severed body part back to "life" and uses it to gain revenge or complete some other objective. These parts can remain unattached or may have been transplanted onto another human. They often belonged to "mad stranglers" in life.

Variants may be powered by science or radiation, but regardless of origin, no psychic zombie is truly undead.

Films featuring psychic zombies are:

- *Mad Love* (1933)
- *The Beast with Five Fingers* (1946)
- *Hands of a Stranger* (1962)
- *Dr. Terror's House of Horrors* (1965)
- *And Now the Screaming Starts* (1973)
- *The Severed Arm* (1973)
- *Demonoid* (1981)
- *The Hand* (1981)

- *One Dark Night* (1983)
- *Evil Dead 2* (1987)
- *Body Parts* (1991)
- *Idle Hands* (1999)

## SCIENCE ZOMBIES

Science zombies can be the mindless kind or those that retain their intelligence (if not their souls). Some are true undead, others only appear that way. Those killed by science zombies stay dead.

In the science fiction films, *Invisible Invaders* and *Plan 9 from Outer Space* (both 1959), aliens use the bodies of the dead to attack humanity. The aliens in *Invisible Invaders* are energy beings that physically merge with corpses, wearing them like "meat suits" in order to interact with the physical world. *Plan 9*'s aliens operate the zombies by remote control "radio waves" from their spaceship. Experimental sonic technology also bring the dead back to life in *The Living Dead at the Manchester Morgue* (1974, aka *Let Sleeping Corpses Lie*).

The 1973 TV movie, *The Night Strangler*, features a Civil War-era mad scientist creating an "elixir of life" from the spinal fluid of beautiful women. The elixir must be injected every 21 years, and has the effect of sustaining the scientist's physical body (as well as giving it super-strength). If he does not receive another dose after 21 years, he begins to age and rot until he crumbles to dust.

Similar to *The Night Strangler*, undead mad scientist Dr. Freudstein sustains his nightmarish existence through alchemy and murder in Lucio Fulci's *House by the Cemetery* (1981). The main difference between these two scientists is The Night Strangler appears human, while Dr. Freudstein is slimy, rotting, and full of maggots.

Depending on when they are revived by mad scientist Herbert West's serum, the zombies in *Re-Animator* (1985) can be anything from violent morons to every bit as smart as they were when alive.

Another example of an intelligent zombie created (at least in part) by science is in David Wellington's novel, *Monster Island*. A medical student in a viral zombie outbreak commits suicide, but takes every possible precaution to preserve his brain function. The experiment works! Although still a flesh-eating zombie, he has retained his personality, emotions, and memories, as well as a high degree of self-control around those tasty humans. He also gains the ability to command other zombies.

## SAMPLE SCIENCE ZOMBIES

- *Invisible Invaders* (1959)
- *Plan 9 from Outer Space* (1959)
- *The Night Strangler* (TV, 1973)
- *The Living Dead at the Manchester Morgue* (1974, aka *Let Sleeping Corpses Lie)*
- *Shock Waves* (1977)
- *House by the Cemetery* (1981)

## VIRUS ZOMBIES

This zombie is the modern, flesh-eating kind. They are the means by which the zombie virus spreads itself, serving as mobile disease platforms. They infect others through biting, clawing, or transmission of bodily fluids. Once infected, a person develops a high fever, sickening and dying within a few days at most. Those who die as a result are reanimated by the virus. They get up (as best as they can, depending on their injuries), and begin wandering aimlessly until they locate food. That food is uninfected humans.

Zombie vision is poor, so they rely on their sense of hearing and smell to track prey. They never tire, so it's impossible to outrun them. You can lose them (so long as you don't run away in a straight line), or trick them into following something noisier or easier to catch. If you are trapped, zombies will try to break in to eat you. If they fail, they'll wait around for you to come out or easier prey to come along.

Zombies have a blank expression, an empty gaze, and show various signs of injury and decomposition depending on how they died and how long they have been dead. They walk with an awkward, shuffling gait that can sometimes (if they are fresh enough) become a short, clumsy run when food is nearby.

Some may use simple tools like rocks or sticks as bludgeoning weapons, or sharp objects like knives, especially if they died with them still clutched in their hands. A rare few who were trained in firearms may remember how to shoot, but not reload, nor will their aim be accurate. For an example, watch *Day of the Dead* (1985).

Generally, the zombie will retain one or two quirks of its former human self. Some may even attempt to do things they did in life, performing skills like drive a car or actions like go shopping at their favorite store. These may give the zombie character, but they don't give it humanity, or true intelligence. They are "ghost behaviors," left-over patterns and impulses that the zombie virus has not yet over-written. On some level, the virus may even encourage these behaviors if they help it find food.

In the initial stages of a zombie apocalypse, zombies will be fresh, and may not appear to be obviously dead. This, combined with no one knowing what a zombie is yet, makes it easy for the virus to spread.

A reanimated zombie initially appears confused, almost as if they are trapped in a dream, but this confusion quickly vanishes, replaced by hunger and aggression. New zombies may also experience flashes of recognition of the people they knew when they were alive; this can result in the zombie hesitating to attack those people (if they loved them). Presented with a choice between someone they loved and someone they didn't, a "fresh" zombie will almost always choose to attack the person they did not know or love. Of course, various factors may prevent the zombie from selecting that person; these could be distance, difficulty, or the interference of the person they know.

Zombies are driven by hunger. They live to kill and kill to eat, infecting as many as they can along the way. Zombies can only be killed by destroying the brain, which is where the virus is centered. A zombie with its head cut off can still bite, a zombie with its legs blown off can still crawl. They keep coming. And they want to make you just like them. That's what makes them scary.

The zombie virus may be man-made, or a natural or supernatural mutation, even a magical curse, but it's origin isn't important. In fact, it's a terrible idea to explain why the dead are rising; no one has ever gotten it right and only looked stupid for trying. That's not to say you can't have characters in your story *try* to explain it, but only as conjecture. No definitive explanation should be given. Trust me, you can't get clever here.

Whatever reason you have for why flesh-eating zombies exist, keep it to yourself. Your readers don't care, and more than that, *they don't want to know*. I'm telling you this as horror fan who has watched virtually every zombie movie ever made. The ones that try to explain it always suck. Instead, just let the zombie apocalypse happen. That's the fun, that's the fear: *Not knowing why*.

## INTELLIGENT ZOMBIES

Intelligent fast zombies can be found in *Return of the Living Dead* (1985); they are created by a military nerve gas. They can talk and reason to a degree, but are in incredible pain, a pain that is only temporarily lessened by eating live human brains (or inflicting pain on themselves, as seen in *Return of the Living Dead 3*). Anyone killed by these zombies or exposed to the gas that created them becomes a zombie.

Another intelligent zombie, if not as fast or smart, is "Bub" from George Romero's *Day of the Dead* (1985). Bub is a standard flesh-eating shambler, but one who has been "domesticated" by a mad scientist and taught to remember pieces of his old human life. As long as he is fed and treated kindly, Bub remains tame and loyal.

A third type of intelligent zombie exists: former zombies "cured" by science (or magic) and restored to life of one kind of another. This concept is explored in the BBC TV series, *In the Flesh* (2013-14), and the films *The Returned* (2004), *Warm Bodies* (2013), and *The Cured*

(2017). What rights do formerly dead people have? Can they relapse into their former savage state?

Some newly risen zombies start off intelligent, but as the rot sets in, so does the savagery. Eventually, they become mindless killing machines. This is explored in *My Boyfriend's Back* (1993), *Boy Eats Girl* (2005), and *Life After Beth* (2014).

Infected people losing their minds as they turn into zombies can be seen in *Colin* (2008), *Contracted* (2013) and its sequel, *Contracted: Phase 2* (2015) and in the "New Year's Day" episode of *Fear Itself* (TV, 2008). A comedy version of intelligent zombies can be seen in *Deadheads* (2011).

## FAST VS. SLOW ZOMBIES

Personally, I favor classic, slow-moving zombies. When you try to make zombies "more extreme," you're just making it harder to suspend disbelief. How does a regular human die and come back to life as an undead track star?

The other problem with fast zombies is it ruins the fantasy. Many zombie fans want to at least *pretend* they have a chance to survive in a post-apocalyptic world. As soon as the zombies run faster then they can, their chances of survival go from slim to none. That may be "extreme," but it's not realistic.

One way around the believability issue of fast zombies is to substitute living maniacs created by a virus instead (see the chapter on Human Monsters for more on "Virus Maniacs" like those found in *The Crazies* and *28 Days Later*).

## SAMPLE VIRUS ZOMBIES

- *Night of the Living Dead* (1968 and 1990 remake)
- *Dawn of the Dead* (1978 and 2004 remake)
- *Burial Ground: The Nights of Terror* (1981)
- *Hell of the Living Dead* (1981, aka *Night of the Zombies*)

- *Day of the Dead* (1985)
- *Return of the Living Dead* (1985)
- *Night of the Creeps* (1986)
- *Dead Heat* (1988)
- *Return of the Living Dead 2* (1988)
- *Braindead* (1992, aka *Dead Alive*)
- *My Boyfriend's Back* (1993)
- *Return of the Living Dead 3* (1993)
- *Cemetery Man* (1994, aka *Dellamorte Dellamore*)
- *Bio Zombie* (1998)
- *Resident Evil* series (2002-16)
- *Shaun of the Dead* (2004)
- *Boy Eats Girl* (2005)
- *Land of the Dead* (2005)
- *Severed: Forest of the Dead* (2005)
- *Fido* (2006)
- *Diary of the Dead* (2007)
- *Flight of the Living Dead: Outbreak on a Plane* (2007)
- *Colin* (2008)
- *Dead Set* (TV miniseries, 2008)
- *Deadgirl* (2008)
- *Fear Itself* (TV, 2008, "New Year's Day" episode)
- *Dead Air* (2009)
- *Dead Snow* (2009)
- *The Horde* (2009)
- *Survival of the Dead* (2009)
- *Zombieland* (2009)
- *The Dead* (2010)
- *Highschool of the Dead* (Anime, 2010)
- *Juan of the Dead* (2010)
- *Rammbock* (2010, aka *Berlin Undead*)
- *Contracted* (2013)
- *The Dead 2: India* (2013)
- *The Walking Dead* (TV, 2011-present)
- *The Battery* (2012)

- *Warm Bodies* (2013)
- *World War Z* (2013)
- *Contracted: Phase 2* (2013)
- *In the Flesh* (TV, 2013-14)
- *Life After Beth* (2014)
- *Wyrmwood: Road of the Dead* (2014)
- *Extinction* (2015)
- *Fear the Walking Dead* (TV, 2015-present)
- *Maggie* (2015)
- *The Rezort* (2015)
- *Seoul Station* (Anime, 2016)
- *Train to Busan* (2016)
- *Cargo* (2017)
- *The Night Eats the World* (2018)

## VOODOO ZOMBIES

Depending on if magic is real in your story, these can be true undead or else the result of being given a dose of *tetrodotoxin*, a neurotoxin derived from puffer fish venom that causes the victim to appear dead. Before death can occur, however, the victim is given an antidote along with a dose of *datura stramonium*, a plant-based drug with strong hallucinogenic and alleged mind control properties. The victim is then convinced by the Voodoo *bokor* (wizard) that he is now not only dead, but a zombie, and his soul has been stolen by the bokor and will not be returned unless the zombie obeys his commands.

Voodoo zombies are used as slaves in Haiti, frequently on plantations either around the clock or as the "night crew," so as not to upset those who work the fields by day. Zombies are created from those the priest hates or desires to control, or from those who won't be missed so the bokor can profit by turning them into zombies.

Voodoo zombies are incredibly hard to kill; they don't feel pain and will attempt to follow whatever the last order they were given until destroyed. Undead zombies are not immortal and will break down over time until they become useless. However, the bokor will get many years (often decades) of work out of them before this happens. If fed salt, Voodoo zombies must return to their graves peacefully and lay down to die; they cannot be reanimated again after this, as it also frees their souls from the bokor's bondage.

Zombies created by drugs are not undead and can be killed normally (though due to their drug-induced state, they ignore pain and keep coming until suffering crippling injury). They may be incapable of coherent speech or precise motion, and may or may not recognize the people they knew in life. They are emotionally flat, speaking slowly if at all. Their brains are hopelessly broken, their will shattered. They exhibit various symptoms of severe mental illness, such as schizophrenia or catatonia. They may not be able to do much of anything for themselves unless ordered to, and are prone to wandering away if left unsupervised.

## SAMPLE VOODOO ZOMBIES

- *White Zombie* (1932)
- *Black Moon* (1936)
- *Ouanga* (1936)
- *Revolt of the Zombies* (1936)
- *King of the Zombies* (1941)
- *I Walked with a Zombie* (1943)
- *Revenge of the Zombies* (1943)
- *Voodoo Man* (1944)
- *Zombies on Broadway* (1945)
- *Voodoo Island* (1957)
- *Voodoo Woman* (1957)
- *Zombies of Mora Tau* (1957)
- *Plague of the Zombies* (1966)
- *I Eat Your Skin* (1971)
- *Isle of the Snake People* (1971)
- *Asylum* (1972)
- *Sugar Hill* (1974)

- *Zombie* (1979, aka *Zombi 2*)
- *Dead and Buried* (1981)
- *The Serpent and the Rainbow* (1988)
- *Voodoo* (1995)
- *Ritual* (2002)

## VIRUS MANIACS

Similar to virus zombies, virus maniacs are living maniacs created by a virus, bioweapon, radiation, fungus, or other mind-altering property or substance, such as the modified strain of LSD ingested by drug test patients in *Blue Sunshine* (1977) or the linguistic "word virus" of *Pontypool* (2008).

Virus maniacs may or may not be able to spread their madness through bites and bodily fluids similar to zombies. Depending on the nature and stage of infection, virus maniacs may look perfectly healthy to obviously ill, all the way to horribly diseased and deformed. The effects of the virus may be permanent or may wear off over time or when certain conditions are met (injected with a vaccine, etc.).

## SAMPLE VIRUS MANIACS

- *Matango* (1963, aka *Attack of the Mushroom People*)
- *I Drink Your Blood* (1970)
- *The Crazies* (1973 and 2010 remake)
- *Who Can Kill a Child?* (1976)
- *Blue Sunshine* (1977)
- *Rabid* (1977)
- *Cannibal Apocalypse* (1980)
- *The Children* (1980)
- *Nightmare City* (1980)
- *Night of the Comet* (1984)
- *Warning Sign* (1985)
- *Primal Rage* (1988)

- *Grindhouse/Planet Terror* (1997)
- *28 Days Later* (2002)
- *Cabin Fever* (2002)
- *The Happening* (2008)
- *The Signal* (2008)
- *Pontypool* (2009)
- *State of Emergency* (2011)
- *Come Out and Play* (2012)
- *Cooties* (2014)
- *Hidden* (2015)
- *The Girl With All the Gifts* (2016)
- *Viral* (2016)
- *The Cured* (2017)
- *Mayhem* (2017)
- *Mom and Dad* (2017)

# 10

# CUSTOM ZOMBIE BUILDER

WE THINK OF ZOMBIES as having a specific set of strengths and weaknesses which vary by type (viral, voodoo, etc.). For example, Voodoo zombies may be blocked by salt, while viral zombies are only destroyed by traumatic brain injuries.

For your convenience when creating new zombies, here is a list of possible zombie strengths and weaknesses:

## POSSIBLE ZOMBIE STRENGTHS

- Bloody Projectile Vomit (five-foot range)
- Can Create New Zombies of Any Type (either as slaves under its control or free-willed)
- Can Create New Zombies of Its Same Type (either as slaves under its control or free-willed)
- Enhanced Physical Perfection (erasing any scars, tattoos, brands, blemishes)
- Enhanced Senses (such as seeing in pitch darkness, hear conversations across a crowded room, etc.)
- Gains victims' memories from eating their brains

- Immortality (may show signs of decay but won't fall apart)
- Immunity to Psychic Abilities (either all or specific)
- Natural Defenses (claws, fangs, poison, etc.)
- Resistance to Pain (either all or specific kinds)
- Resistance to Psychic Talents (either all or specific)
- Spread Disease through Bodily Fluids or Wounds
- Super-strength
- Super-reflexes
- Super-speed

## POSSIBLE ZOMBIE WEAKNESSES

- Cannot Consume Normal Food/Drink (becomes ill)
- Cannot Enter Holy Ground
- Cannot Climb or Swim
- Comatose During the Day
- Killed by Traumatic Brain Injury
- Hurt or Killed by Decapitation
- Hurt or Killed by Dismemberment
- Hurt or Killed by Fire
- Hurt or Killed by Holy Objects
- Hurt or Killed by Salt
- Hurt or Killed by Sunlight
- Must Feed on Brains (can be animal or human)
- Must Feed on Flesh (can be Animal or other non-human)
- Must Feed on Flesh (must be Human)
- Repelled by Fire
- Repelled by Holy Objects
- Repelled by Salt
- Repelled by Water

Remember, anything a zombie is drawn to can be used against it. Clever (or desperate) characters could use the zombie's favorite food as bait or poison.

# 11

# DISASTER PLOT TEMPLATES

## THE RACE AGAINST TIME AND THE HOLE-UP AND HOLD OUT

WHETHER NATURAL OR MANMADE, disasters have always fascinated us because they aren't science fiction—they're science fact. Climate change, asteroids, volcanic eruptions... all can create apocalyptic scenarios, and in mere moments, paint a post-apocalyptic landscape.

There are basically two types of plots for disaster stories: The Race Against Time and The Hole-up and Hold Out (similar to the Siege). The first type of plot involves scientists, the military, law enforcement, or other emergency preparedness personnel in a position able to avert, divert, or mitigate the impending disaster. The second type of plot is the exact opposite, and deals with regular people caught up in and attempting to survive impossible situations... perhaps in an unusual location, such as a ski resort, high rise, bomb shelter, on board a speeding train, on the last flight out, etc.

Eventually, both plots end or morph into post-apocalyptic plots: either The Road, The Siege, or both (these are discussed in the next chapter).

You can replace zombies with looters or crazed survivors, nukes with tornadoes, volcanos, hurricanes, a nuclear power plant melt-down—whatever disaster you like! The disaster can be all on its own or as a side effect of nuclear war, zombies, aliens, crazed robots, etc.

The two disaster plots can be combined with each other and/or with the post-apocalyptic plot. This is typically done by having a married couple split between two locations: one relatively "safe" and other very much in danger. One spouse is the professional racing against time, the other has no clue what to do and is just trapped somewhere, relying on others for survival. As long as the two can communicate, you have a bridge between the plots, but at some point, that communication must be cut off. This typically as soon as the danger hits, shortly before, or shortly after.

When you combine disaster plots with post-apocalyptic ones, you create new and interesting variations on the end of the world. For example, *Flight of the Living Dead* (2007) takes the classic airport disaster movie and combines it with zombies for a fresh spin on the apocalypse. Can they land the plane safely? Should they? Or will the Air Force shoot them out of the sky to contain the infection?

*Train to Busan* (2016) is zombies on a train, which *The Cassandra Crossing* (1976) did as a straight virus movie forty years earlier.

What classic disaster movie plots can you combine with the end of the world? The possibilities are endless...

In particular, I want to point out one low-budget apocalyptic gem, *This is Not a Test* (1962). It's a tense one location drama, like *Night of the Living Dead*, but without zombies. It deals with a group of people stuck on a lonely desert highway on the night World War 3 begins. The would-be survivors are caught between a brutal deputy sheriff with orders not to let anyone pass his roadblock, and an escaped serial killer posing as a hitchhiker. You can guess how things turn out...

## SAMPLE DISASTERS

- *Deluge* (1933)
- *In Old Chicago* (1937)
- *The High and the Mighty* (1954)
- *A Night to Remember* (1958)
- *The Last Days of Pompeii* (1959)

- *The Day the Earth Caught Fire* (1961)
- *This Is Not a Test* (1962)
- *Crack in the World* (1965)
- *Airport* (1970)
- *The Poseidon Adventure* (1972)
- *Earthquake* (1974)
- *Heatwave!* (TV, 1974)
- *The Towering Inferno* (1974)
- *The Hindenburg* (1975)
- *The Cassandra Crossing* (1976)
- *Two-Minute Warning* (1976)
- *Avalanche* (1978)
- *Blackout* (1978)
- *Beyond the Poseidon Adventure* (1979)
- *The China Syndrome* (1979)
- *City on Fire* (1979)
- *Meteor* (1979)
- *Plague* (1979)
- *Goliath Awaits* (1981)
- *The Day After* (TV movie, 1983)
- *Starflight: The Plane That Couldn't Land* (TV, 1983)
- *Runaway Train* (1985)
- *Daylight* (1996)
- *Night of the Twisters* (1996)
- *The Trigger Effect* (1996)
- *Twister* (1996)
- *Dante's Peak* (1997)
- *Titanic* (1997)
- *Volcano* (1997)
- *Hard Rain* (1998)
- *Armageddon* (1999)
- *Deep Impact* (1999)
- *The Perfect Storm* (2000)
- *The Core* (2003)
- *The Day After Tomorrow* (2004)

- *Poseidon* (2006)
- *Blackout* (2008)
- *2012* (2009)
- *Knowing* (2009)
- *Aftershock* (2012)
- *The Impossible* (2012)
- *It's a Disaster* (2012)
- *Pompeii* (2014)
- *San Andreas* (2015)
- *The Wave* (2015)
- *Cordon* (TV, 2016)
- *Deepwater Horizon* (2016)
- *Geostorm* (2017)
- *Only the Brave* (2017)

Now that we've got a grasp for the scope and kind of disasters we can write about, let's explore how to put them in practice with my convenient disaster plot templates. These work for any pre-apocalypse, early stage apocalypse, or contained (limited scope) apocalypse.

## "THE RACE AGAINST TIME" PLOT TEMPLATE

1. We briefly meet the main character(s) in their Ordinary World before they have any news of an apocalypse. We see their hopes, their reality, their flaws. They go about their normal day, which gives us a chance to meet most of the supporting cast along with any minor characters.
2. Suddenly, they get the news the apocalypse is coming. This news typically comes down the chain of command from their superior, or a close, highly-placed contact if the main character is at or near the top of their particular food chain (mayor, chief of police, etc.). The news may be vague or specific at this point, but even if it is presented as the complete picture, it will not be.

3. A hurried meeting is held and amidst much tension, ideas, theories, and strategies are presented, rejected, and accepted. This is an opportunity to see the main character shine, as well as any rivals or villains on the team to reveal themselves.

4. The main character is assigned an important task to complete in relation to the disaster, but not given enough time, people, or resources. This creates more tension, more desperate hope that somehow, some way, it will be enough. It has to be.

5. News of the disaster (or its side effects, such as looting) reach the main character. This incentivizes him to hurry in his task.

6. A breakthrough is discovered, and implemented, but the calculations are off, data faulty, etc. What was supposed to be a triumph turns into a disaster. Violence and other loss ensues.

7. Back to the drawing board. More ideas, more theories, more strategies are discussed, but now they have even less time, people, and resources. Things look bleaker than ever.

8. The main character snaps out of his depression... something he heard earlier, some vital piece of information that seemed unimportant at the time, suddenly comes back to him in a "Eureka!" moment.

9. The discovery is met with resistance, if not outright rejection, by the main character's superiors or colleagues (especially any rivals or villains). Time is running out. Another plan is put forward by a rival or villain and accepted.

10. The main character goes behind the back of his superiors and implements his own plan by whatever means necessary. Violence may ensue.

11. As the rival plan fails, the main character comes forward with his plan, which is either ready to go, or already in effect, and after more tension, his plan is fast-tracked,

receiving additional people and resources. The rival or villain, seeing no other choice, may reluctantly join forces with the main character at this point, or else bow out of the project. Then again, they may try to stop the main character, leading to violence and other loss. Perhaps a supporting character, an ally of the main character, is killed or injured in the conflict.

12. The main character's plan achieves success, though not without cost—more cost than if his superiors had listened to him in the first place. The extent of that success is limited to provide the author's desired outcome. Likely only a portion of humanity is spared the disaster, but a larger share than would have been spared otherwise. The story usually ends on a bittersweet but hopeful note, though of course, you're free to end it however you like.

## "THE HOLE-UP AND HOLD-OUT" PLOT TEMPLATE

1. We briefly meet the main character(s) in their Ordinary World before they have any news of an apocalypse. We see their hopes, their reality, their flaws. They go about their normal day, which gives us a chance to meet most of the supporting cast along with any minor characters.

2. Suddenly, they get the news the apocalypse is coming. This news typically comes from the media or an unreliable third party. As such, the news is vague, misinformed, or outright propaganda at this point, but even if it is presented as the complete picture, it will not be. The news may be scoffed at and dismissed or taken seriously. This is when a "ticking clock" countdown to disaster kicks in, whether the main character knows it or not.

3. Regardless of whether the news is believed, something happens to make the main character aware that something strange is going on, so it's better to be safe than sorry.

4. The main character gets in contact with friends and family to try to a) corroborate the story, b) check on their welfare, and c) to see if they should coordinate on some kind of shared survival plan. They will put together some sort of vague, badly thought-out plan on the fly.

5. The main character travels to gather supplies and encounters tension, violence, and other unsuspected frightening events that foreshadow the impending disaster and the worst of human nature.

6. The main character is threatened at this point and one or more strangers comes forward to intervene, driving off the threat and displaying their fighting competence and/or empathy. This impresses the main character so much that the stranger(s) are invited to join in the survival plan. The stranger(s) agree. The stranger(s) should be chosen to provide skills the main character lacks and to fulfill whatever role you need: lover, warrior, strategist, rival, enemy, etc.

7. The characters collect—or attempt to collect—the other people and/or supplies in the plan. This should lead to more tension, and possibly violence. Possibly new characters are added to the group at this point, and these are the ones most likely to end up as rivals or villains.

8. With as many people and supplies as they can manage, the characters beat a hasty retreat to their hold out location. Something goes wrong. Maybe a flat tire, a road block, looters or other criminals, or somebody forgot something important and decides to go back and get it, promising to see them at the hold out later... which may or may happen.

9. The characters hole up in their hold out, erecting what defenses and other safety precautions they can. Windows will be boarded up, etc. Something will be found (or found out) that appears inconsequential now but will take on great importance later.

10. The countdown to the disaster approaches the end. If they

were not aware of the countdown before, they are now, either from obvious signs outside or through the media or online. Tension mounts. This is a good time to insert a sex scene, a fight, or both.

11. The disaster hits, preferably at the climax of the sex, fight, or whatever tense moment you've selected. The story can end here if you don't want any survivors. Otherwise, everyone goes into shock or panic. Some bounce back faster than others, some may never bounce back and this can be a problem later as these characters will be either useless or dangerous to the group.

12. The survivors decide on a new plan based on the disaster. The plan sounds logical—and it may be—but because the characters are lacking certain vital information, it ends up getting one or more of them killed.

13. The survivors regroup and come up with more ideas and theories and strategies, leading to more tension and possibly violence. At this point, whatever item or news you planted earlier that was ignored is now seized upon by the main character and presented to the group; this act quickly diffuses the tension and/or end the violence. The group has hope again.

14. The characters decide to act on the new plan and achieve success, though not without cost. If you are running a hybrid plot with the Race Against Time template, this is where the couple are reunited. The story can end here on a bittersweet but hopeful note, or as a tragedy, or it can morph into one of the post-apocalyptic plots: either The Road or The Siege. Which one depends on whether the group has kept or lost its shelter.

## 12

# POST-APOCALYPTIC PLOT TEMPLATES

### THE ROAD AND THE SIEGE

NOW THAT YOU KNOW how to start your story, what about the plot? Well, good news! There are only two main plots in post-apocalyptic fiction: "The Road" and "The Siege." Some stories find a way to combine the two, such as *The Road Warrior* (1981) or *The Walking Dead* (TV, 2010-present), while others may use only a little of one and a lot of the other.

For example, your story could start with the characters on the road seeking permanent shelter—a journey that takes up most of the story—only to find it but be besieged and lose it all. The survivors end up on the road again...

Or, your story could begin with your characters holed up in what they *think* is a permanent shelter, fending off siege after siege until they are forced to go on the road.

Both plots prove nowhere is safe in the end. And that's the point of writing post-apocalyptic fiction: *What you think will save you will kill you if you hold on too tightly.*

If you are writing a story with monsters other than zombies, you can still use these templates. Simply swap in whatever type of creature you want: aliens, animals, mutants, road warriors, robots, vampires, etc. They all work.

## "THE ROAD" PLOT TEMPLATE

1. The apocalypse strikes suddenly or is already underway (this choice determines how knowledgable your characters are about the threat).
2. Your characters are on the road or quickly end up there. They either have a "safe" destination in mind or are actively looking for one. If not everyone knows each other, this is the place to reveal more about them—both to deepen their relationships and to lay the groundwork for schisms you can exploit later. Alternately, a loner hero may wish to stay on the move, one step ahead of trouble.
3. Other survivors show up seeking similar resources or shelter; these people can be friendly or hostile. If they appear useful, the characters' group further argues and schisms over whether or not to let the new people in. One of the new people is wounded. If infected, they become a secret (or not so secret) threat, depending on if they reveal the wound was caused by a zombie or not.
4. The characters seek shelter and supplies, encountering various obstacles and clues to an alleged "promised land." Their group suffers attrition through fighting internal and external threats but hangs onto a glimmer of hope—just enough to keep going.
5. The characters find the "promised land" is not all it's cracked up to be. Either it is abandoned, overrun, damaged, or occupied by hostile or unfriendly forces. The characters must find a way to make the shelter work by repairing it—or, if it is already inhabited, by proving themselves to the occupants or defeating them.
6. The shelter now *appears* "safe" and the characters allow themselves to relax. This is where you contrast the characters' new way of life from their one on the road. This is a prime place to slow things down by exploring and

deepening the characters' relationships—as well as their schisms. Any unrevealed back stories, secrets, or traumas go here.

7. Factions within the group that had previously held together in the face of external threats now have an opportunity to fight for dominance. This fight directly or indirectly leads to the group being unprepared for the siege.

8. If there is still power and access to media, the characters may use TV, radio, or internet to get more information—that information could lead to more conflict within the group as they argue over what should be done with it. If the news says a better shelter is available nearby, some of the group will leave at this point (either by sneaking out and stealing vital weapons and supplies, or on amicable terms, promising to send back help).

9. More survivors show up seeking the same shelter; these can be friendly or hostile. If they appear useful, the characters' group further argues and schisms over whether to let the new people in or not. One of the new people might be wounded. If infected, they become a secret (or not so secret) threat, depending on if they reveal the wound was caused by a zombie or some other contagious disease.

10. Zombies and/or hostile human forces (possibly following the new arrivals) besiege the shelter.

11. The characters must decide to stay and fight (and likely die) or flee back to life on the road. Not everyone will believe the situation is hopeless, and some may stay knowing it is suicide, but are willing to sacrifice themselves to help the others escape.

12. Those who stay either die or manage to survive and flee or restore security to the shelter. Those who flee either live and face an uncertain future or are killed in the process. Neither the characters who stay or the ones who flee may know what happened to the other group. It is OK to leave some doubt as to the fates of both groups in the reader's

mind, but most stories will show the fate of one, implying they will survive—for now.

## "THE SEIGE" PLOT TEMPLATE

1. The apocalypse strikes suddenly or is already underway (this choice determines how knowledgable your characters are about the threat).
2. The characters begin in a "safe" or "safe for now" shelter or quickly find one as the world crumbles around them. If not everyone knows each other, this is the place to reveal more about them—both to deepen their relationships and to lay the groundwork for schisms you can exploit later.
3. Since the characters are stationary, other than events in their immediate vicinity, the greater collapse is often illustrated through watching TV, listening to the radio, or phone and internet connections as long as the power lasts. The information the characters receive will be fragmented and often wrong or out-of-date, full of deliberate or unintentional misinformation, and paint a far rosier or blacker picture depending on the news source. If your story takes place in modern times, internet information will be all over the place in terms of quality. Every crazy or malicious weirdo will be on social media spouting vitriolic, panicked nonsense that will get the people who listen to it killed or worse. If the characters are influenced by outside advice or "facts," this may cause them to abandon their current shelter. If they do, this becomes "The Road" plot. If they stay, "The Siege" plot continues. Either way, you want your characters to argue and discuss the information they are receiving and what they should do about it. This creates a schism in the group you can exploit later.
4. The characters run low on supplies and decide to get more by mounting scavenging or raiding parties that send them

further and further from their shelter as time goes by and the surrounding areas are picked clean. The characters might need general supplies or specific ones like a certain type of medicine.

5. Other survivors show up seeking the same shelter; these can be friendly or hostile. If they appear useful, the characters' group further argues and schisms over whether to let the new people in or not. One of the new people might be wounded. If infected, they become a secret (or not so secret) threat, depending on if they reveal the wound was caused by a zombie or some other contagious disease.

6. Zombies and/or hostile human forces (possibly following the new arrivals) besiege the shelter.

7. The characters must decide to stay and fight (and likely die) or flee back to life on the road. Not everyone will believe the situation is hopeless, and some may stay knowing it is suicide, but are willing to sacrifice themselves to help the others escape. Those who stay either die or manage to survive and restore security to the shelter. Those who flee either live and face an uncertain future or are killed in the process. Neither the characters who stay or the ones who flee may know what happened to the other group. It is OK to leave some doubt as to the fates of both groups in the reader's mind, but most stories will show the fate of one, implying they will survive—for now.

Notice that "The Siege" plot has twelve steps and the "The Road" only has seven. That does not make it easier to write! If anything, it makes it harder, because much of the Siege ends up being like a one-room stage play.

In a Siege, if you write yourself into a corner, you don't have the luxury of saying the characters just "move up the road to see what's next." The Road is a *proactive* plot, while the Siege is *reactive*. The people won't leave their shelter unless they're absolutely sure that's the right move. That means you have to get more creative giving them a reason to leave. And of course, a "good reason" to one character will be a "bad reason" to another. So they will argue and waste time until one side wins, or until hostile forces make it impossible for either side to stay.

Remember that these templates are *guidelines* to help you construct a satisfying plot, they aren't meant to restrict you. Think of it like a recipe: some people like certain spices, others don't. Some like a pinch, some like a heaping spoonful. Season your plot to taste.


## HIT THE EASY BUTTON

You can move the template plot points around if you want. Or, you can cut or combine some. And you can always add more. *In particular, plot points 9-10 in The Road (5-6 in The Siege) can be repeated as often as needed.* Throwing more survivors and/or hostiles into the mix can help get your plot back on track. It can also squeeze in some much needed action to pick up the pace.

As hardboiled author Raymond Chandler said in his famous essay, *The Simple Art of Murder:* "When in doubt, have a *man* come through the door with a *gun* in his hand."

You can substitute the words "man" and "gun" with *anything*. For example, "When in doubt, have a *zombie* come through the door holding a *severed head* in his hand." Or, "When in doubt, have a *woman* pull a male character aside and tell him *'We need to talk.'*" Now that's scary!

Don't let too many chapters go by without your characters at least seeing, hearing, or thinking about the threat they're facing. It doesn't have to be a fight, but the threat must be present in some way. For example, placing zombies as menacing sounds or shadows in the distance can drive home your otherwise safe character's increasing loneliness and isolation.

Have one of the characters go crazy. By "crazy," I don't mean foaming at the mouth, full-on axe murderer crazy. I mean give them a *temporary* psychotic break where the stress they're under freaks them out enough that they make bad decisions that could get the group killed. They may have to be restrained, knocked out, killed, or banished. Or maybe they unlock the back door when no one is looking and run away, leaving it open behind them—and in walks the villain and his henchmen, or some zombies...

You can also hit the easy button with any villains or traitors that are already within the shelter; have them hatch a plot to take over the group, deny others important resources, or attempt to get away with something selfish or nasty. They could hoard food, ammo, information, anything. Maybe they do it not to be a dick, but simply because they don't trust the main character and want to be sure they have some "holdout" supplies in case things go badly. The end result is pretty much the same regardless of their intentions: a fight that's verbal, physical, or both.

Feed the characters new information from a "trusted source" either through the media or a character they meet. After a brief argument/discussion, this information sends the characters in a new direction—and into new danger. Is the source of the info compromised by a villain? Or is it just plain wrong, misguided, or out-of-date? Maybe it's a prerecorded message on a loop and when the characters get there, they find the promised shelter abandoned or held by hostile forces.

Remember, if something sounds too good to be true, it usually is—but in the apocalypse, you'll still have plenty of survivors ready to believe anything that gives them hope...

# 13

# SURVIVAL HORROR

MORE PLOT IDEAS AND TIPS

WHEN YOU ADD ZOMBIES, monsters, or other survival horror elements into your plot, there are a few things to be aware of. Remember you can replace the word "zombie" with whatever type of villain or creature you want. You can also replace "apocalypse" with "disaster" or "invasion." Zombies may be the most common survival horror story, but they are by no means the only one, especially outside the post-apocalyptic genre. Films like *Alien* (1979) and *Aliens* (1986), *Predator* (1987), *Cabin Fever* (2002), and *'Salem's Lot* (TV miniseries, 1979) are all about surviving, whether against aliens, disease, or vampires.

## THE FIRST NEWS THE APOCALYPSE HAS BEGUN

For pre-apocalypse stories, you need to be careful how you dispense the information the danger is coming. You don't want to just blast it out in the first few pages or even the first chapter (unless you are writing a short story). That's called an "info-dump" and readers hate it. Instead, you want to spoon feed clues, slow and steady.

The characters should never have the whole story in the first few chapters. Tease them with traffic accidents, distant screams or sirens, shadowy figures shambling in the distance, odd but not overly alarming news reports, missing person flyers on telephone poles, that sort of thing. Build mystery and suspense now, while you still can. The horror will come soon enough.

## THE FIRST ZOMBIE SIGHTING

Note that a sighting does not mean an attack. In a pre-apocalypse setting, the first time the characters see a zombie, it should be ambiguous as to what it is. They should think the zombie is alive, that they're simply drunk or sick or crazy. When possible, keep the zombie at a safe distance, one step removed from the characters so there is no way the zombie can immediately attack. The zombie may be preoccupied and not even notice the character. What's important is that the character notices the zombie, wonders about it briefly, then moves on with their life.

Honestly, this "zombie" could just be a drunk or homeless weirdo. That part doesn't matter. What matters is we plant the *idea* of zombies in the readers' mind. The character, on the other hand, remains oblivious, which builds suspense.

If you begin your story in the pre-apocalypse, you have 25 pages at most to reveal the first "zombie" sighting (which could be someone who is merely infected but not yet turned, or a drunk or crazy person as previously suggested) and 50 pages to bring on the first zombie attack. If you can't get to the zombie action in the first 50 pages, you're probably telling the wrong story—one that will bore and annoy zombie fans.

If you begin during or after the apocalypse, you only have 10-15 pages to show the first zombie and 25 pages to begin the first attack because *expectations are different*. Once our society is in a state of collapse, you expect to see zombies pretty damn quick.

This rule more or less applies to screenplays too, regardless of whether they are pre-, during, or post-apocalypse. That's because each page in a screenplay translates to an average of one minute of screen time. Most movies are only 90 minutes, so they need to move faster than fiction.

Due to the variable length of short stories, change the above page counts to the *percentage* of story. So by 25% of the way in, you'll have revealed the first zombie sighting. By 50% of the way in, you'll hit the first zombie attack. In a short story, it may not always be possible (or advisable) to have more than one zombie attack, so choose it carefully—both *when* it happens and *what* it consists of.

Not every story needs a ravenous horde of undead. You could get by with just a few zombies, or even one, as long you do two things:

1. Imply there are more lurking around; and
2. Use the ones you've got to maximum effect.

In the film *It Stains the Sands Red* (2016), there is only one main zombie, but this works because it takes place in the Nevada desert. It's logical there's only a few undead around, and only one doggedly pursuing the heroine.

## THE FIRST ZOMBIE ATTACK

The first zombie attack should come as a complete surprise to the character(s). It must be terrifying, not horrifying. What do I mean by that? I'm going to paraphrase the Alfred Hitchcock definitions: Terror is when the audience knows there is a bomb set to go off under a table two men are sitting at. They talk in a casual, friendly manner, neither having any idea they are about to die. But the audience knows, and the audience fears for them. *That is terror.*

Horror is when the bomb goes off and we see the men die, their limbs flying, their faces blasted off. In a zombie story, the fans *want* horror, they expect and demand it, but they *need* terror if you want them to remember your story as something other than a mindless gore-fest.

The entire opening to *Night of the Living Dead* (1968) is devoted to setting up its first zombie attack, and does so in the smartest way possible:

A brother and sister drive to an old cemetery to lay flowers on their father's grave. They tease and argue with each other about the drive, about how they should move the grave closer to their homes, why they don't have any candy left, etc. Through this sibling banter, we get to know and care for the two characters, Barbara and Johnny.

Slowly, Johnny realizes the empty cemetery frightens his sister, so like any good older brother, he tries to spook her. Barbara gets angry.

Meanwhile, in the background, we see what looks like a drunk weaving his way between the tombstones. Johnny uses the man's shabby appearance to further frighten his sister, and in a nice bit of foreshadowing, tells her, *"They're coming to get you, Barbara... Look, here comes one of them now!"* He laughs and runs a short distance away to watch his sister embarrass herself.

As expected, Barbara tries to apologize for her brother's childish behavior. The man attacks her. Great Scott, he's a zombie! Johnny rushes to the rescue but the zombie kills him, then chases Barbra until she takes shelter in a not so empty farm house.

More survivors and zombies arrive. The Road part of the plot is over. The Siege begins.

This opening works because we spend time getting to know Johnny and Barbara. We like them, even if Johnny's an ass and Barbara's prim and uptight. They feel like real people, going about their lives. If the film had not spent the time it did establishing the characters and their relationship, then no matter how gruesome, the horror would have been "who cares?" instead of "holy shit!"

It's one thing to say, "watch the movie," and another to say "now write a novel." So let's take a look at how to do that with the novelization of *Night of the Living Dead*:

At dusk, they finally spotted the tiny church. It was way back off the road, nearly hidden in a clump of maple trees, and if they had not found it before dark, they probably would not have found it at all.

It was the cemetery behind the church that was the objective of their journey. And they had hunted for it for nearly two hours, down one long, winding rural back road after another with ruts so deep that the bottom of the car scraped and they had to crawl along at less than fifteen miles per hour, listening to a nerve-wracking staccato spray of gravel against the fenders and sweltering the a swirl of hot, yellow dust.

They had come to lay a wreath on their father's grave. Johnny parked the car just off the road at the foot of a grassy terrace while his sister, Barbara, looked over at him and breathed a sigh intended to convey a mixture of happiness and relief.

Johnny said nothing. He merely tugged angrily at the knot of his already loosened tie and stared straight ahead at the windshield, which was nearly opaque with dust.

— John Russo, Night of the Living Dead

There's lots of scene setting here to drive home the rural isolation. We know there won't be any help coming when something goes wrong... Anyway, after some sibling drama, Johnny and Barbara lay their wreath, then the villain appears... the first of many, only Johnny and Barbara don't recognize the danger they're in.

In the distance, a strange moving shadow appeared, almost as a huddled figure moving among the graves.

Johnny and Barbara dismiss the "strange moving shadow" as the caretaker, and go on arguing. About the past. About the present. And soon, none of it matters, because the man is there, and he's not the caretaker at all. He's a walking corpse!

And suddenly, the man grabbed Barbara around the throat and was choking her and ripping at her clothes.

Johnny comes to his sister's defense, but only succeeds in getting himself killed. Barbara runs off in a panic, pursued by the shambling zombie. She locks herself in an isolated farmhouse that becomes surrounded by the living dead!

Although Barbara doesn't die, she does descend into a near useless, semi-catatonic state. The real hero, Ben, shows up and sets about trying to save them both. It's up to him to explain what's going on and the nature of the enemy—as well as how to destroy them. That's important.

Johnny and Barbara are victims. Victims don't understand what's going on at first, and that's as it should be. This sets the stage for the hero to come in and look like he knows what's going on and what to do.

If you'd like to study more on the subject of throwaway victims, I recommend reading the *Novelist's Essential Guide to Crafting Scenes* by Raymond Obstfeld (chapter 10).

## WHAT DO THEY KNOW BEFORE THE ATTACK?

In a pre-apocalypse situation, the characters will have no information and therefore no idea how to deal with that first zombie. Make the reader feel the character's fear, confusion, and anger. Make the first zombie attack not so much about physical violence, but *emotional violence.*

The first attack should completely terrify the character, ripping them out of their comfort zone and providing a taste of the horror to come. With later attacks, you can let the gut-ripping begin. Remember, if you go over-the-top too early, you have nowhere to go later. Don't set yourself up for failure. Deliver the gore the fans expect, but *delay gratification* as long as possible. That makes the gore more special, more horrifying than if you just serve it up as an "all you can eat" buffet.

During the apocalypse, the characters will have *some* information, but still may not believe the dead are coming back to life or that the government won't somehow save the day. They are still tied to the old ways of thinking, to their old lives. They must wrestle with that even as they struggle to adapt to the rapidly changing (and worsening) situation. They must learn the old rules don't apply anymore, and let that be as painful a lesson as possible.

Even in a post-apocalypse world, don't underestimate the power of a good scare. Characters used to dealing with zombies can still be surprised by encountering them in an unexpected situation. They can still be terrified, you just have to try harder.

## QUICK ZOMBIE APOCALYPSE PLOT IDEAS

Stumped? Here's some ideas to get your juices flowing:

✓ A mysterious illness falls over a rural town; the people who die from the virus don't turn into zombies, but the ones who got sick and survived do!

✓ A conspiracy-loving hero begins to see signs of the zombie apocalypse *and* a government cover-up. He tries to warn the world but no one listens.

✓ Government troops quarantine a town infected with the zombie virus. They claim they are there to help, but they are really conducting a secret weapons test.

✓ Bodies are found partially eaten, but no one believes the town drunk that a "zombie" did it.

✓ Soldiers lost in the desert are stalked by zombies created by a chemical weapons.

✓ A mad scientist devises an experiment to bring his dead friend/family/lover back to life. An unexpected side effect is the reanimated person is an *asymptomatic* carrier of the zombie virus.

✓ The military reanimates the dead as super-soldier bio-weapons. They retain their memories and organize an escape that spreads the infection.

✓ A human lures a zombie horde to seek revenge on the group that kicked him out of his own shelter.

✓ Heirs invited to the reading of a will at a secluded country estate are slowly dying. A greedy murderer wants the fortune all for himself, but every person he kills becomes a zombie. Think Agatha Christie's *10 Little Indians* (1943) meets *Burial Ground* (1981).

As you can see, there are all kinds of ways to personalize your apocalypse story. Taking hit films or genres and mixing them with zombies is a good way to do it. That's where "zom-rom-coms" like *Shaun of the Dead* (2004) and *Pride and Prejudice and Zombies* (2016) came from. Even *Star Wars* novels jumped on the zombie train with Joe Schreiber's *Death Troopers* and *Red Harvest*. See? Zombies can boldly go anywhere you want.

Another idea to elevate your story and make it "high concept" in Hollywood terms is to do something new and different with zombies. A recent example is *Cooties* (2014), which takes place in an elementary school where only the kids turn into zombies. Zombie children are rare but not new. It's the school setting that makes it different. Other zombie kid flicks include *Who Can Kill a Child?* (1976) and its 2012 remake, *Come Out and Play*, as well as *The Children* (1980), Stephen King's *Pet Sematary* (1989), and *Wicked Little Things* (2006).

## THE FOREIGN ZOMBIE APOCALYPSE

Almost every zombie movie has been set in the US or UK. But what would the apocalypse look like in a different country, specifically in the early stages?

In *What We Become* (2015), we see how Denmark falls. *The Grapes of Death* (1978) and *The Night Eats the World* (2018) show zombies in France. *Burial Ground* (1981) takes place in Italy at an Etruscan villa and adjacent monastery.

In *The Dead* (2010), we see how the virus affects Africa. And in the sequel, *The Dead 2* (2013), we watch it spread across India, which is also the backdrop for *Go Goa Gone* (2013). *Train to Busan* (2016) and its animated prequel, *Seoul Station* (2016), show a fast-moving zombie apocalupse in Korea. *Battle Girl: The Living Dead in Tokyo Bay* (1991), *Junk* (2000), *Versus* (2000), and *Stacy: Attack of the Schoolgirl Zombies* (2001) all have wildly different takes on zombies in Japan.

Older films like *Zombi 2* (aka *Zombie*, 1979) show flesh-eating zombies on a Caribbean island, while *Zombi 3* (1988) and *Zombies: The Beginning* (2007) take place in the Philippines. The jungles of Papua, New Guinea are the location of *Hell of the Living Dead* (1980, aka *Night of the Zombies, Zombie Creeping Flesh*).

Exotic locations can add a fun flavor to your story, making even simple interactions complicated if your characters are unfamiliar with the local customs, language, and area.

## THE EARLY OR CONTAINED APOCALYPSE

Not every zombie story has to be about a major apocalypse, or at least not a world-wide one. *28 Days Later* (2002) and its sequel, *28 Weeks Later* (2007), initially only had their "Rage" virus affect the UK. I know some horror fans might want to correct me here that the "Infected" from these films are still alive, not undead. And you're right, but they look and act like zombies, so that's good enough for me.

You can narrow down the affected area of your apocalypse as much as you want, from the world to a country, a state or province, a city, a small town, even a rural area. Look to films like *The Andromeda Strain* (1971), *The Crazies* (1973/2010), *Outbreak* (1995), *[REC]* (2007), *Quarantine* (2008), *What We Become* (2015), and series like *The Strain* (TV, 2014-2017) and *Cordon* (TV, 2016) for examples of how federal, state, and local government deal with a small-scale quarantine situation. Everything they do will be focused on containment, while those trapped inside will be focused on breaking out before they get infected too.

The plot templates still apply, but you now have a bit more wiggle room. Forces of law and order still exist. You even have a chance for a happy ending, if that's what you desire. Whatever caused the outbreak could still come back, as it did in *28 Weeks Later*, when the UK quarantine was lifted and they tried to rebuild the shattered country. This led to new infections and this time, the Rage virus leapt past the borders to infect other countries.

## NON-APOCALYPSE ZOMBIE PLOTS

Most of the ideas in this book center on traditional flesh-eating zombie plots in a contemporary setting with an accompanying apocalypse of one magnitude or another. But what if that's not the story you want to tell? What if you're using Voodoo or Demonic Zombies? What if they don't have an infectious bite?

That doesn't mean you can't use The Road plot, but it needs tweaking (see below). The Siege plot, however, can work pretty much "as is." Again, you get a bit more wiggle room because the forces of law and order still exist. But what if the evil wizard controlling the zombies is also the mayor? Or in some other position of power? He could be a ruthless industrialist intent on turning the local population into undead slave labor. He could be a mad scientist running zombie mind control experiments out of his clinic.

The point is, the early or small-scale apocalypse and the non-apocalypse plots are almost always a *mystery* or *thriller* plot first and a survival horror Siege second.

What's the difference between mysteries and thrillers? In a mystery, the characters might know what's going on but they don't who's responsible. This is a *proactive* plot where the villain reacts to the actions of the characters. In a thriller, the characters know (or think they know) what's going on and who's responsible. Thrillers are a *reactive* plot driven by the actions of the villain; the characters in it are stalked, chased, threatened, and worse by the villain.

To put it another way, the characters control the direction of the mystery, and the thriller controls the direction of the characters. It's important to get that right.

*Murder on the Orient Express* (1974) is a mystery. *The Bourne Identity* (2002) is a thriller. Want to add zombies to them? Watch *Horror*

*Express* (1972) for a weird murder mystery with zombies on a train. For a zombified Jason Bourne movie, simply have him doing covert ops during the apocalypse and/or replace his normal enemies with trained undead or mutant assassins. It would then become much more like the *Resident Evil* film series (2002-2016).

With a limited or non-existent apocalypse, there is simply more time for characters to wander around looking for clues or to convince the authorities of the danger. There is still some sense of "safety" and hope for survival. Only when the forces of law and order have been fully compromised or destroyed does The Siege plot begin.

Alternately, once the shelter is rendered non-viable and the local area unsafe, you could switch to The Road plot. That is, if you want to show that the evil has spread to adjacent areas.

# 14

# STARTING YOUR STORY

## INCLUDES WRITING EXERCISES

WHERE TO BEGIN? This is a question only you can answer. There is no right or wrong way to begin your story's timeline, whether it be pre-apocalypse, during the apocalypse, or post-apocalypse. Each offers distinct advantages and disadvantages that must be carefully weighed before making a decision: Start too early, and the reader is bored waiting for the end of the world to begin. But start in the middle of an attack, and the action is meaningless because the reader doesn't care about the characters yet. As with any type of story, *balance is key*.

## ✓ PRE-APOCALYPSE

Depending on how interesting and revealing you can make it, it may be advisable to begin the story showing the main character (or multiple characters) in their Ordinary *Pre-Apocalypse* World. What were they doing before the apocalypse touched them? What were their hopes and dreams? What kind of people were they? Who or what did they lose in their life before the apocalypse? This determines what kind of survivors they will be, and influences every other stage of the plot.

## ✓ DURING THE APOCALYPSE

If you choose to begin your story *during* the apocalypse (before civilization has fallen), then you need to show the characters operating in their Ordinary *Apocalyptic* World; this presents the most options for wild change from scene to scene as the situation is rapidly shifting. Characters may be safe one chapter, doomed the next, then saved again, etc.

## ✓ POST-APOCALYPSE

If you choose to begin your story *after* the apocalypse, then you need to show your characters operating in their Ordinary *Post-Apocalypse* World to establish their normal before moving on. This gives the reader a chance to adjust to the story world and get to know the characters before any major action commences. If you fail to establish the characters and setting, even briefly, any action you insert won't work because the reader doesn't care yet.

## HOW TO WRITE KILLER OPENING LINES

Maybe you've read my best selling book, *Writing Dynamite Story Hooks*, a guide to crafting story hooks (opening lines and entire first chapters). If you haven't, I recommend you read it before starting your story. It's easy lessons and killer strategies apply to any fiction genre.

But I'm not going to make you buy another book just to use this one, so my basic advice is keep your first sentence short and punchy; insert your main character's name if possible. *Don't* start with weather or setting, but *do* tease us with something exciting and/or mysterious. Examples using different points of view (POV) might be:

- Derek Mason aimed his rifle out the attic window.
- Tiffany Loomis had never seen a dead body before.
- Jan Clark was jogging when the ambulance shot by.

- Something about the patient disturbed Mike Kelly.
- I swerved around the screaming man.
- I'm walking home from school when the bombs drop.

Notice how each example grabs the reader? They do that to accomplish two tasks:

1. Instantly orient the reader to the viewpoint character (which can be the main character or a "throwaway" victim if you prefer).
2. Planting a mystery in the reader's mind to create the expectation of action and horror to come.

It doesn't matter if you're using third person or first person (either in past tense or present tense). You can even use the unpopular second person POV if you want:

- You aim your gun at the dead man.

See? POV doesn't matter. All of these are fantastic first sentences. *Short and sweet.* There's no room for confusion, no chance to get bored. These lines achieve this by gently *easing* the reader into the story. They also raise reader expectations you are an author who knows how to deliver.

If this is your first book, you can't help being a newbie, but you don't have to make the same mistake so many new authors do. *You can absolutely have a first-class opening line in your first book.* In fact, it's essential that you do if you're going to stand out.

As best selling author Mickey Spillane put it, *"Your first line sells the book. Your last line sells the next book."*

## HOW TO WRITE KILLER FIRST PARAGRAPHS

Make sure your first line sings, then start polishing the first paragraph, the first page, the first chapter. So how do you do that? The first line sets up the action, but you can't rush into it. Remember, the reader doesn't care about your character yet. You have to pull back, give them a broader understanding of what they read in the first line.

Here's an example from one of my zombie short stories:

> Veronica and I are fighting over a boy again. We don't even know his name, but pickings are slim after the world ended. Everyone is in a hurry, but not us. We stand on the street corner, waiting for something to happen. *Or someone.*
> — from "Two Girls, a Guy, and the End of the World"

See how this example begins with the characters taking action? The main character and her friend are fighting over a boy and they've done it before. But do we find out who he is or witness the details of the fight yet? No. Instead, I use the opportunity to pull back and explain the setting (post-apocalypse) and location (a street corner). I take the time to briefly convey the present emotional state of the characters (bored, desperate, hopeful). Only *after* I accomplish these goals do I bring the boy in and put the girls' fight in context.

This is much more effective than starting with the fight. Why? Because now the reader knows who is present, what they are doing, and why they are doing it. We also get that all-important first glimpse into their thoughts and emotions; this gives readers a feel for what kind of story this will be. The other advantage of holding back the boy is I can focus on just two characters instead of three.

Let's take a look at expansions of my earlier examples to see how I might build them into gripping first paragraphs:

> Tiffany Loomis had never seen a dead body before. She thought maybe it was a joke, some kind of Halloween prank. She looked around wildly, scanning the thick bushes lining the street for kids waiting to jump out at her. She saw no one.

> Jan Clark was jogging when the ambulance shot by. It nearly hit her, and she fell into a ditch scrambling to avoid it. The ditch was muddy

with last night's rain, ruining her expensive new jogging suit. Before she could even get to her knees, another ambulance sped past, followed by a patrol car. All of the vehicles had their sirens blaring. Jan watched the receding taillights, wondering what was going on.

Something about the patient disturbed Mike Kelly. He'd only been on call a few hours, and the night shift at Lincoln Memorial was never this busy. As Mike bent to inspect the injured man, he caught a whiff of rot coming from the wound. He didn't need to be a doctor to know it was a bite mark.

I swerved around the screaming man. He was in the middle of the road waving his hands, begging me to stop. To help. And I could have, but that would be breaking the rules Terry and I lived by: *Don't stop. Don't help. Don't trust. Not anyone. Not ever.* It's how we'd stayed safe during the apocalypse. Well, safe until last night. We'd broken the rules and Terry paid the price. Now she was gone.

I'm walking home from school when the bombs drop. I can't believe what I'm seeing: the orange sky, the mushroom clouds. It's hell on earth. And here I am worried about the "F" Mr. Wilson gave me on my math test. Whether to lie or tell my parents. I've got something else to tell them now, if they haven't seen it already. If they're even still alive.

I whipped these paragraphs up in just a few minutes. I don't say that to brag, but to prove you can do it too. It's easy once you get the hang of it and I'll show you how.

Before we get to those writing exercises, Let's try one more first paragraph, this time using the second person POV:

You aim your gun at the dead man. You're waiting to see if he gets up again. Waiting to see if he's like all the rest who died but didn't stay dead. You have to be sure because this guy isn't like the others. *He's your father.*

You have to start with a bang, pull back, then hit them again with the last line of your first paragraph. *BAM!* No escape. They're hooked. They have to keep reading.

You do this by teasing your readers, tempting them, then delaying gratification as long as you can (but not too long). It's all about pacing.

*Pacing controls suspense.*

## WRITING EXERCISES (Do Not Skip!)

1. Pick a character name, profession, and location, then stick that character in their Ordinary World as they confront an unusual situation. Give yourself no more than five minutes to brainstorm the best first line you can, then allow yourself another five minutes to expand that line into a first paragraph. Use a timer. Don't stop to revise or edit.

2. Do this as many times as it takes to internalize the process. I recommend at least five times total, using a different character with a different profession in a new location and situation each time.

3. Now reread the paragraphs you've just written and analyze them to see what works and what doesn't.

4. Feel free to revise and edit them all until you're happy—but don't spend too much time on this. You don't want to slow your progress. Think of yourself as a shark: You have to keep swimming or you drown. Whatever doesn't get fixed now can get fixed in the next draft.

Besides teaching you the skills to start your story in the best and most interesting way possible, this exercise has a baked-in bonus: How many first paragraphs did you write? That's how many beginnings to future novels and short stories you've written. Sure, you may not use them all, but if you use even one, you're ahead of the curve. Next time you want to start a story, grab one of these babies and you're up and running.

Or, if you're feeling ambitious, you could even use several of these first paragraphs to introduce characters *in the same story*. You'll still need to flesh out the rest of their introductory chapters and decide how they'll meet. You'll also need to figure out their relationships to each other (if any) and whether their roles as survivors will be as heroes, sidekicks, traitors, villains, or victims.

It's wise to pick a character from the supporting cast to be the "stakes character" (a lover, friend, or family member) that the other survivors can rally behind either to rescue or avenge. You don't need more than one stakes character and having more than one only dilutes the importance of each.

To learn more about stakes characters, heroes, villains, anti-heroes, and supporting cast, read my best selling book, *Writing Heroes & Villains*.


## HOW TO WRITE A KILLER FIRST CHAPTER

To create your first chapter, simply keep doing what you've been doing. Start strong, end strong. Make us like (or at least be amused or interested by) your main character. Build tension. Avoid back story. Drop hints to the past, but save any lengthy explanations for chapter 2 or 3. Otherwise, you will bore your reader by slowing the pace of that crucial first chapter with a bunch of information no one needs yet.

With short stories, you have more flexibility since you have to fit the same information into fewer pages. But the basic rule still applies: *Don't rush it.* Don't front load your story with boring shit. Whatever is in the first chapter must earn its place or it has to go. So either cut it completely, or move it to later in the book.

If you're still in doubt, switch your chapter one with chapter two and see if that doesn't fix any pacing problems.

What about prologues? Don't do it! Many people hate prologues and skip reading them because too many bad authors chose to slap a "spoiler" or some boring nonsense on the front of their books for the past decades. If you still insist on a prologue, *don't call it that*. Call it anything else: "Before," "Thursday, 7 a.m.," "Patient Zero," etc. Hell, if none of those work, call it "Chapter 1." Just be sure you can't tell your story without it. Otherwise, cut it.

To help you see behind the scenes of my creative process, I've included a case study containing the complete first chapter of "My Own Decisions," a zombie story I wrote for my extreme horror collection, *Gore Girls*. The extensive footnotes explain how and why I made each and every decision as an author. Analyzing my first chapter will help you better write your own in a way that will satisfy readers and sell more books.

**15**

---

# ZOMBIE STORY CASE STUDY

(FOOTNOTES APPEAR AT THE END OF THIS CHAPTER)

**MY OWN DECISIONS**

Jackson Dean Chase

DEREK MASON AIMED HIS RIFLE out the attic window.[1] He was picking targets in the street[2] while my big sister, Marnie,[3] rubbed his shoulders and whispered encouragement.

"There's one," she said. "Shoot that one!"[4]

It must've been a hundred degrees in here. No air conditioning, no cool drinks, nothing to make the end of the world any less sweaty and miserable. I sat in the corner with my hands over my ears, waiting for Derek to pull the trigger.[5]

The rifle roared.[6]

My parents were banging around downstairs shoring up our defenses.[7] They were always mad about something, but the gun noise really set them off. I wasn't a fan of it either. It attracted zombies[8] from the street toward the house, and that was never good. Still, at least it wasn't the other sound—the one I had to listen to all night of Derek and Marnie making out behind the bed sheet they'd hung to get some privacy. Like I really cared to spy on that! Well, OK, I'll be honest—I didn't mind looking at Derek, especially with his shirt off, but not when he was doing stuff with my sister.[9]

*I wanted him doing that stuff with me.*[10]

Derek was the best-looking guy my sister had ever brought home.[11] What he saw in her, I'll never know, but Derek was a catch. His eyes were sexy-blue and his hair was blonde and styled just right. Or it used to be. Now it was all greasy from days of brutal heat and no showers,[12] but he didn't seem to mind. He'd wink and smile, and at least try to be nice to me. Not like my sister, who was always bitching about something. Mostly me.

The end of the world[13] hadn't done much to improve my relationship with Marnie. Especially once we got stuck in the attic. Not only had she kept her big sister authority over me, but when our parents decided to stay downstairs—"to make sure we were safe," were their exact words—Marnie acted like she was my mom. Even before the apocalypse, she was always telling me to shut up, or go away, to stay out of her clothes and makeup. It seemed like the only time Marnie liked talking to me was to rub her boyfriend in my face.[14]

"Derek is so handsome," she'd say, or, "Maybe someday you'll get a boyfriend, Lisa—if you don't scare him off with that mousy brown hair and scarecrow-thin body of yours. You're like a human coat hanger."[15]

I'd study myself in the mirror and wonder what was taking so long, why I didn't look all curvy and round in all the right places like her. "Maybe someday" better come soon, because I'm not sure how much longer I have to live. I hoped it would be long enough to get a boyfriend, even if we could never go to the prom or the movies or do anything normal. At least we'd have each other.

I looked over at Derek again, hunched over the windowsill, rifle pointing into the street. What if everyone else was dead? What if Derek was the last guy on earth? I bit my lower lip and another "what if" popped into my head, something so horrible it made me excited and ashamed all at the same time: *What if something happened to my sister?* Would Derek stay with me? Would he finally see in me what he saw in Marnie?[16]

No way, I thought. No guy wants a "coat hanger" for a girlfriend. Not if he has a choice. Plus, Derek's totally seventeen. He's gonna graduate next year and go off to college with Marnie and I'll never see him again. Only wait, I forgot there won't be anymore graduations. No more school, no nothing. There was only this attic and whatever world we made from it.

The rifle cracked, ear-splittingly loud in the dusty confines of the attic.[17]

"Omigod!" I said, coming over to the window where Derek and Marnie were fooling around with Dad's rifle. "Would you guys please stop? You know Mom and Dad hate noise."

Marnie looked at me like I was retarded. "It doesn't matter what Mom and Dad hate anymore," she said. "We're up here, and they're down there. I'm in charge. Besides, Derek and I are practicing."

"Oh," I said. "Practicing what? How to get us killed?"[18]

"Check it out," Derek said. He made room for me to see what he was up to.[19]

I peeked out the window. I didn't much like looking outside anymore, not since the dead started coming back to life. It was pretty gross seeing strangers walking around all dead and rotting, but friends and neighbors were the worst. Like old Mrs. McGruder next door, who'd been like a grandmother to me, but now walked around in circles on her front lawn with half her face chewed off.[20] Or that cute boy, Eric Westin, who lived two houses over. He'd been my first kiss last summer when I turned thirteen.

It hadn't worked out with him, thanks to stupid Angela Overton, who'd stolen Eric from me a week later with her overdeveloped chest and big fat ass.[21] No, I wouldn't be making out with Eric again, and not just because he was a zombie. Angela still had him, and they were undead together, all vacant-eyed and drooly-mouthed.

I saw them now, stumbling up and down the street, holding hands like it still mattered. Nothing much mattered, but at least they had each other and that was something.[22]

What did I have? A smelly attic, a few days worth of food and water,[23] and a sister who hated me. There was no place to plug anything in here, so the batteries to my iPod had died and the only sounds I got to hear everyday were Derek and Marnie sucking face,[24] Mom and Dad banging around, and whatever weird groans came from the zombies outside.

"I got one!" Derek said. "See that?" He pointed at the body of a UPS guy and grinned. "Total head shot."[25]

He was right. The delivery man's brains were all over the pavement, steaming in the August heat.

"Derek got him on the second try," Marnie bragged. "A few more shots like that, and he's gonna get us out of here."

I pushed Marnie out of the way and took her place by his side.[26] "So what's the plan? You gonna shoot all those zombies?"

"No," Derek said. "I don't think I'll have to. They're pretty slow, and we can probably get around them without wasting too many bullets. I just wanna get a feel for the gun, is all. I haven't had a chance to use it since..."

"Since you borrowed it from Dad," I answered for him. "I remember."

Derek and Marnie exchanged a look—one of those secret looks they were always giving each other. They didn't think I noticed, but I did. They were planning to ditch me, make me wait here with Mom and Dad while they got help. *If they got help.* Or maybe they planned to never come back. It's not like I could read minds or anything, I just knew they were up to something and didn't like it.[27]

I grabbed hold of the barrel and pointed it toward Angela Overton. "Shoot her! I bet you can't hit her."[28]

Almost as if she could hear me planning her murder, the dead girl stopped in the middle of the street and stared at us. Most of her once-graceful neck had been chomped off by Eric, but she managed to tilt her head enough to let us know she was on to us. Eric stopped shuffling too and looked in our direction. Only Mrs. McGruder kept moving, still in the same slow, lazy circles. She didn't respond much to anything anymore, but then she'd always been hard of hearing.

Marnie yanked me back, out of sight from the street. I took a few steps, fell, and hit my shoulder on the chest of old junk we'd moved over the trapdoor.[29] It led to the downstairs hallway near my bedroom.

Marnie said, "Sorry, Lisa, but you know you're not supposed to make noise."

I rubbed my shoulder and glared at her from where I sat sprawled next to the chest. "Oh yeah? Well, what about that rifle, huh? It's not exactly quiet, you know."

"That's different, Lisa. We need to learn how to use it if we're gonna get out of here."

"When are we doing that? Before or after the food runs out?"

"Before," Derek said. "Now can you two stop fighting so I can finish practicing?"[30]

Marnie apologized, but returned my glare. She was always apologizing to him, so much you'd think she couldn't do anything right. But it made Derek happy, so I guess it made sense.

"Yeah," I echoed. "Sorry, Derek."[31]

Derek stuck the gun out the window. I came back over, wedging myself next to Derek's left side while Marnie stayed on his right. But it made Derek happy, so I guess it made sense.

"This one's for you," he told me.

I followed his gaze into the street. Angela's head disappeared in a pink mist of scrambled blood and bone,[33] and it was the most romantic moment of my life. I think I loved Derek then.[34] I threw my arms around his neck and hugged him, planting a sloppy kiss on his cheek.[35]

Marnie rolled her eyes. "Jeez! It's only a zombie. Don't make such a big deal out of it."

In the street below, zombie Eric tugged at his fallen girlfriend's lifeless arm, not realizing she couldn't walk with him anymore. He kept tugging until her arm tore loose. Eric wandered off with it, trailing gore.[36]

An angry thump came from downstairs. Mom and Dad were pissed.[37]

~

LATER THAT NIGHT, after a dinner of cold pork and beans and warm Diet Pepsi, Marnie said she felt sick[38] and went behind the curtain to rest. That didn't bother me, since it left me alone with Derek. As alone as we could be in a one-room attic.

"I wanted to thank you for shooting that girl today," I said. "She was really bugging me."

Derek shrugged and bit into a Snickers bar. "Had to shoot one of 'em," he said. "Might as well make you happy at the same time, right?"

"Yeah. Hey, can I have some of your Snickers?" "Take it." He handed me the candy bar.

I took a bite, realizing I was tasting more than chocolate, caramel, and peanuts—*I was tasting him.*[39] It wasn't the same as making out, but it was the closest we'd ever gotten. I wondered if Derek knew that? Was that why he handed me his candy bar? Was it some secret boy way of reaching out to me? I could barely see him in the deepening gloom. There were no more candles, so there wasn't much to do after dark except sleep, and dream of Derek...

I handed him back the bar. "Here, you finish it."

He took it and ate the rest. I watched him do it, trying not to giggle. I'd kind of slobbered on it, but he didn't seem to mind. Maybe because he knew what I'd done and liked it, or maybe because it was the last one. Either way, a little bit of me was in Derek now.

We sat in the dark, listening to the creepy moans from the street, not saying much. The streetlights had been off since yesterday, but the moon was full. It was almost romantic, but then I had to ruin it by asking, "How come Mom and Dad are always making noise?"

Derek turned away from me. "I told you, they're boarding the doors and windows to keep us safe."

"But shouldn't they be done? It's taking forever, and I wanna recharge my iPod, take a shower, and get some more clothes and stuff."

"The power's out," he said. "Your parents told us to wait here."

"Yeah, but I don't understand why Mom and Dad don't come up to check on us."

"Look," he said, "they're fine, all right? They're busy reinforcing the barricade. All the doors and windows have gotta be perfect, or else—"[40]

Marnie sighed in her sleep. She'd been kind of sick lately, vomiting in the morning and being more irritating than usual. I'd asked if she was pregnant, but she'd given me this weird look and said, "Mind your own business."[41]

Derek looked in Marnie's direction. "I should check on her. "Goodnight, Lisa."

"Wait," I reached over and put my hand on his knee.[42] "I, uh, wanted to say thanks for being here and helping save me and stuff. You're really awesome."

"No problem. I'm glad I could be here for you and your sister."

"And our parents," I added. "You're helping them too."

"Sure," Derek said. He moved away, and then he was hidden behind the blanket. With her.

I could hear the two of them whispering, then the slow, soft kissing sounds began.[43] I closed my eyes and tried to pretend it was me he was kissing, but it didn't work. I put my hands over my ears and turned away.[44]

## FOOTNOTES

1. The first sentence gives us the character's name, location, and that he's taking a dangerous action. It also combines action with mystery. We don't know if Derek is a hero or villain or what he's aiming at.
2. The second sentence increases suspense by expanding on the dangerous action.
3. After increasing suspense, another character is introduced taking an action that adds mystery. Why is Marnie

encouraging Derek to shoot? Who or what are the targets in the street?

4. Dialogue is used to ratchet up the suspense even more.

5. Just when we think Derek is ready to pull the trigger, we delay reader gratification by introducing a third character (and the hero/narrator), who is less concerned about shooting than her comfort. To introduce her after Derek shoots would be a mistake. We need to know she's there so we can get her reaction both before and after Derek pulls the trigger. I don't recommend introducing more than three or four characters on the first page or you'll clutter it up and it will feel rushed.

6. After delaying gratification by introducing the narrator, we cut back to action. You want to delay gratification to increase suspense, but not so long readers lose interest. Once you set up the action, don't delay more than a page or two. (Note the action is set off on its own line to stress its importance.)

7. After having Derek shoot, we now delay gratification again. Why? Because we can! There are two more characters (the parents) we need to introduce. Since they weren't in the attic and unaware of what was happening, we don't need their reaction before the shot is fired, only after

8. After keeping the reader in the dark for several paragraphs, we now reveal the "targets in the street" are zombies. This means the characters in the attic are survivors, not villains, and we can begin to empathize with them. The mystery is solved. Of course, we'll be setting up another soon.

9. Now that the action and mystery are resolved, we can take a moment to establish the relationship between the characters. You must do this as quickly as possible after introducing them.

10. Now jealousy is revealed as the reason why the narrator doesn't want Derek to be with Marnie. This creates

suspense of a different kind. What is the narrator going to do about her problem?

11. We get insight into Derek's good looks and disparaging remarks about Marnie's attractiveness. Both filtered through the jealous lens of the narrator, who is proving to be rather unreliable.

12. Now we get confirmation of the story's timeline. They've been trapped for days, but I don't just say that, I *show* it through the effect the weather and passage of time is having on Derek's hair. This not only provides the necessary information, but again drives home how important superficial things (looks and comfort) are to the narrator.

13. The fact the zombie apocalypse is worldwide and no help is coming is revealed here as no big deal compared to the worsening relationship between the sisters.

14. Be careful with backstory in chapter one. This is a short story, so I can get away with it here, but in novels, backstory is often better placed in chapter two.

15. Now we get a brief description of the narrator and seeming evidence Marnie is mean to her, but can we really trust this information from an unreliable narrator?

16. The narrator has her first idea of how to solve her problem. She doesn't jump to murder yet, but to letting the zombies solve her problem for her. That idea won't work because heroes (and I use that term loosely here) must solve their own problems to make for a satisfying ending. If I let zombies eat Marnie without the narrator instigating it, I would be failing my readers. Better yet if I don't let the zombies do the narrator's dirty work and instead force her to kill Marnie herself. By the way, this story is a tragedy if you haven't guessed it already. A tragedy is any story where the hero fails to change. That doesn't mean they win. Winning is usually what happens to heroes who change, but as long as they change for the better, it's okay if they lose. For example, Rocky Balboa in the first *Rocky* film.

17. That's enough backstory. Back to zombie-killing action!

18. The conflict between the characters now comes out as a dialogue exchange.

19. Derek again plays peacekeeper between the sisters, ending the argument by distracting them with the results of his latest shot.

20. Here we reveal the narrator is squeamish, something she'll have to overcome if she's going to kill Marnie. Give your hero quirks and flaws, and especially contradictions, just like real people.

21. Mirroring is a technique where you present another version of the characters and their problem. Here I use it to show the narrator has lost a boyfriend to another girl before, thus mirroring her situation with Derek and Marnie. Although it's more of a distorted funhouse mirror since Derek and the narrator have never been together. It's enough that the narrator wants to be with Derek to make the mirroring work. This adds to her motive to kill Marnie.

22. More motive to kill Marnie. The narrator desperately wants to be loved.

23. Here I slip in details about dwindling supplies, again dismissed as less important than the narrator's relationship with Marnie.

24. Mirroring the "drooly-mouthed" zombies, Eric and Angela, in the street.

25. And back to action. See how I keep cutting back and forth? This time, I pay it off with a dead body.

26. The narrator takes this action not just to get a better view, but because it's subconsciously what she wants to do: replace her sister in Derek's eyes.

27. Another mystery is established. Is the narrator right, or is she delusional? The reader is unsure.

28. The narrator tries to gain control of her situation and ease her feelings of abandonment by forcing Derek to shoot zombie Angela, the girl who stole her first boyfriend.

29. If Mom and Dad have made the downstairs safe, why is the chest blocking the trapdoor? Why haven't we seen or heard more from the parents yet? Another mystery!
30. Derek again tries to keep the peace, but there will be consequences.
31. More mirroring, this time grudgingly.
32. The sisters are now mirroring each other, making it clear through body language they both see him as theirs.
33. Giving zombie fans what they want: gore! It's vital you deliver on reader expectations while still giving them a little twist to keep your story fresh.
34. Derek screws up by doing what the narrator wants. He does it to keep the peace, but instead this action drives the narrator over the edge from mere jealousy to murderous insanity.
35. More mirroring: "drooly-mouthed," "sucking face," and now a "sloppy kiss." This descriptive pattern indicates the narrator wants to physically consume Derek. She's a bit zombie-like herself: single-minded, impossible to reason with. She just keeps coming until she gets what she wants!
36. This is not just gore for shock's sake. This is mirroring the misguided love and loneliness the narrator feels, as well as foreshadowing the scary length the narrator will go to get and keep Derek.
37. More mystery. What's up with the parents? Is it something Derek and Marnie aren't telling the narrator? And if so, why are they holding back this information?
38. Another mystery. Why is Marnie sick? Ostensibly from the food, but what if that's not it? Could she be infected with the zombie virus? Or is it something else?
39. The narrator is officially crazy at this point, making connections that aren't there based on what she wants to be true. "Tasting him" also reinforces her disturbing, zombie-like nature.
40. This dialogue exchange deepens the mystery of the absent

parents. Note that I don't give away the answer here, but let the mystery hang. In chapter two, I use a flashback to reveal the truth, but keep the narrator in the dark because she is missing key information. I also explain her insanity. If this were a novel, I would delay at least some of these reveals longer.

41. The mystery of Marnie's illness is answered here, a page after I raised the question. Any sooner would have been stupid. Always keep readers in suspense as long as you can.

42. The narrator's action of placing her hand on Derek's knee is her subconscious way of physically claiming Derek in a way that a) gives her the illusion of control, and b) sends a signal she's attracted to him that she hopes Derek will pick up on.

43. This time, the narrator refers to making out in a normal, non-zombie like way because, while her passion for Derek is violent and all-consuming, *what she really wants* is quiet, tender love. Deep down, the narrator knows she's too broken to experience that, and she resents Marnie for having it.

44. The chapter ends on a downbeat note because the narrator fails to get what she wants. Try to vary each scene and each chapter so the narrator "wins" in one, then "loses" in the next. This creates suspenseful pacing.

# 16

# HOW TO WRITE DESCRIPTIONS OF ZOMBIES

GOT WRITER'S BLOCK? The following descriptions are taken from the *Post-Apocalypse Writers' Phrase Book* by Jackson Dean Chase. In it, you'll find over 4,000 radioactive ways to describe weapons and wounds, road warriors, ruined cities, robots, aliens, mutants, and much, much more!

Over 200 zombie-related ones are included here:

## PLAGUE

- The plague fell like a shadow across the land
- The government told us it could never happen here
- The government claimed they were close to creating a vaccine
- Men in hazmat suits swarmed into the building
- The hospital staff had never seen any disease like it
- The news said it was a weaponized form of ebola
- The cities fell fast, but rural areas like ours remained relatively safe
- The superbug went airborne, mutating past all our defenses

- Everyone wore masks in public to avoid infection
- The first case appeared on the east coast in April
- The plague was the perfect enemy: silent, invisible, deadly
- The contagion was too virulent to be anything other than man-made
- The scientists had created a new form of life—and a new form of death
- The germs were in the air, the water, there was no escape
- Humanity had been replaced as the dominant species by a virus
- The government secretly infected millions through fake flu shots
- We sealed our doors and windows with plastic, waiting for it to pass
- Every surface had to be disinfected
- Corpses lined the streets waiting to be picked up for disposal
- They dumped the dead into pits and set them on fire
- The dead had to be burned quickly, there was no time for ceremony

## DEAD BODIES

- A bloody hand clawed out of the pile of bodies, clawing at air
- All around were the dead and dying, blood-spattered and broken
- A gore-caked corpse congealed in the corner
- Blood-smeared and shabby, the corpse was clad in old rags
- The shriveled remains were as forgotten as the victim's name
- That there were no visible wounds made the death more suspicious
- A ragged hole in the dead man's neck left no doubt as to

cause of death

- The frozen bodies were stacked like cordwood
- The corpse was a blasted husk in which no trace of soul remained
- There was a look of terror etched on that awful face
- The stench of the dead man's loosening bowels hit me
- The smiling corpse looked as if she had jumped into death's arms willingly
- The bodies lay blackened and burned to ash
- The corpses were grim reminders of what might have been
- The basement was a cobwebbed horror of stacked bodies and secret hell
- The dead girl's flesh was alive with maggots
- Worms crawled over her lips like lovers
- A lone gray worm wiggled its way from the dead man's nose
- The girl was long dead, her body ripe with rot
- Her body was pregnant with the putrescence of death
- The dead man hit the ground with a sickening thud
- Of the original victims, only the heads remained
- Their bodies were propped, as if in prayer
- His blood was still, his heart stopped
- He had died as he had lived
- A soul-blasted corpse regarded him with unseeing eyes
- The grisly remains bore mute witness to the horror she now faced
- The body was rife with corruption
- Without limbs or head to match, the torso was unidentifiable
- A maniac had stitched the bodies together in a mismatched patchwork
- The corpse glared at me, daring me not to join it
- The dead were discarded mannequins, silent and immobile
- Inspecting the bodies, nearly every kill was a head shot
- The butchery was indescribable
- The bodies no longer resembled anything human

- The skeleton leered at her from its hiding place
- The dry heat had mummified the body rather than decomposed it
- They dredged the bloated body out of the lake
- The body washed ashore two days later, a bloated nightmare
- The fish had eaten away the eyes and most of the face
- The crabs had clawed away most of the face-meat
- The body lay in the field, stinking of opened guts and empty promises
- A scalpel had razored her bloodless lips into a grin wider than life
- The corpse's face had frozen in a terrified scream
- The mouth was impossibly wide and horrible in that shriveled face
- The gory remains greeted me as I walked in the door
- Buzzing flies hung like a halo over the corpse's head
- Flies crawled on the congealed ruin of her mangled body
- The hollow-eyed corpse grinned back as if making a joke
- A fat fly crawled over the corpse's ruined cheek
- Hungry maggots oozed out of putrid flesh
- Squirming minions of madness, the blind maggots ate
- The crawling things of the earth covered her like a living blanket
- Maggots feasted on the rotten remains
- Plump, juicy maggots bore holes in him, drilling for the oil of death
- The corpse in the coffin looked strangely at peace
- Even stretched out on the autopsy table, her beauty was undiminished
- The coroner cut into the corpse, searching for secrets
- Bodies in zippered black plastic were ushered into the ambulance
- The paramedics hefted the body into the waiting ambulance
- The body-filled morgue was cold and stank of antiseptic

- The pathologist pulled the steel drawer open, revealing the victim
- Dead or not, the unnatural state of the bodies unnerved me
- In death, as in life, I could not face her
- Bodies draped under sheets greeted me like old friends
- The victim's remains lay on the autopsy table, ready for inspection
- The corpse had the distinctive scars of an autopsy

## ZOMBIE GORE AND MORE

- Shambling hordes of hungry horrors descended on us like locusts
- They were undead eating machines that left nothing in their path
- With strangled cries and haunted faces, the mob lurched forward
- A lone straggler shambled into view, his face a ghastly ruin
- The shuffling of dead feet on broken glass alerted me to their presence
- The air was alive with hunger and nothing else
- It moaned and moved toward me
- Moldy lips peeled back from broken gums
- The thing was missing most of its face, but still it would not die
- A blood-caked abomination crawled into view, its lower half gone
- Creeping, crawling, the creatures came on, horrible in their hunger
- Blood drooling from mangled lips, she shambled forward
- The wind blew the stench of rotting meat ahead of them
- A low, frustrated moan came from the attacker
- I could hear the slow, soft shuffle of dragging feet on broken glass

- His clothes were badly torn, like pack of wild dogs had been at him
- A puckered hole in his neck bent and widened as he turned toward us
- The flesh tore with a wet, sucking sound
- Ghouls feasted on the remains
- Motor control wasn't the creature's strong suit
- The eyes were milky-white, clouded over
- The zombie's eyes saw only the nameless hunger of the dead
- The lips pulled back from the gums, revealing cracked yellow teeth
- She hissed softly and shuffled in my direction
- The zombie whined in surprise to find its prey snatched away
- It tried to clamber through the wrecked door
- It wanted to stuff my face into its putrid, slobbering mouth
- Little by little, the bloody strip of meat vanished between its teeth
- The monster ate his face like the main course at a four-star restaurant
- Growls of frustration followed me as I ran from them
- She sank her bloodstained teeth into the living meat
- Her teeth ripped off a hairy hunk of his arm
- The zombie's eyes closed in ecstasy as it chewed noisily on the entrails
- The unkillable cannibals howled and surged to the sound of my voice
- The pasty-faced ghoul scrabbled after me, biting at air
- The cannibal dead cried out for blood in the language of the grave
- Her unholy fingers curled into claws
- I awoke to the sound of pounding fists and breaking glass
- Bullets knocked some of the sick people down, but they kept getting up
- He was moving fast for a dead guy, closing the gap with

long strides
- Its fingers splayed out, questing for my flesh
- The lower-half of its jaw was sheared away
- The faceless ghoul's tongue licked at lips that were no longer there
- Grime-covered hands clawed at my leg as its beady eyes glared up at me
- The creature's mouth gaped wide, eager to devour
- A half-dozen ghouls ran forward and yanked at the trailing guts
- It shoved the girl's arm into its mouth and bit down—hard
- The flesh-hungry mob batted the air and growled
- The swarm surged in all directions, an endless line of teeth and claws
- Dozens of hungry ghouls pressed into the gap
- Sticky, infected fingers smeared blood and bile across the window glass
- Her jaws snapped shut spasmodically, trying to gnaw through the glass
- He hissed through the pulsing ruin of his ripped-out throat
- The zombie charged forward on unsteady legs
- More zombies—shadows in the moonlight—spilled out of the store
- The ghastly horde closed in, intent on eating them alive
- The ghoul exploded on impact like a blood-filled water balloon
- His chest was a raw wound I could see through
- Gore-guzzling ghouls gaped and moaned
- The flesh-ripping feast had begun
- It was an orgy of toxic hunger
- The infected horror shambled to meet me, ghastly lips drooling gore
- It chewed into her neck with a savage grinding sound
- The hungry corpse bit down, drawing blood
- The dead creature's jaws clamped shut on my arm

- It was ripping and tearing at a piece of bloodied flesh between its teeth
- The ravenous undead swallowed its meal and came back for more
- The gut-ripping horror got up on jerky legs and staggered toward me
- The zombies were a shambling mass of mindless hunger
- The diseased army of death staggered, shambled and crawled
- Infected spit and gnashing teeth came up to meet me
- His eyes were murky, the life bleached out
- The shambler with the missing jaw led the pack in my direction
- The creep with the oozing eye socket blindly staggered forward
- The zombie mob moaned in frustration as I ducked back out of sight
- Hungry eyes and half-rotten faces leered back at me
- The milling mass of hungry dead made it impossible to go forward
- The city streets were choked with smashed cars and living dead
- The street was teeming with the walking dead
- The dead came pouring out of every car, every building
- A crowd of zombies pulled him from the wrecked car, tearing him apart
- A blood-red rain drooled from its crimson lips as it fed
- The zombie's teeth came away glistening with their scarlet prize
- The dead thing gnawed on her body, sucking up the last of life's juices
- The zombies grew smaller and smaller in our rearview mirror
- There were too many zombies to fight
- The rotting dead kept coming until there was no escape

- They were living corpses that fed on death
- A thousand slack-jawed Satans stared up at him
- Their hungry mouths promised damnation
- Intestines leaked from him in a hopeless tangle of doom
- The dead clutched frantically at the exposed intestines
- Steaming ropes of blood-smeared intestines spilled through his fingers
- The first yellowish loops of intestine squirmed from the wound
- The first ghastly worm of intestine peered from the gaping hole
- Blood and bile broke free from the wound–her guts were soon to follow
- Frantic fingers clutched and clawed at her mutilated belly
- Pulled apart, all he could do was die
- The zombie's teeth snapped down on her manicured fingers
- The head tumbled away from the spurting stump
- Blood spilled from the wound in a relentless red rush
- The arm tore free from the shoulder with a sickening crunch
- He yanked on the dangling limb, twisting it free from its socket
- The eyes burst and black fluid gushed
- The zombie's head disappeared in a red mist
- Blood and brains burst out of his shattered skull
- The first slug shredded the trachea just at the hollow of her throat
- The bullet smashed through the bridge of his nose, pulping brain
- The back of his skull burst open like a ripe melon
- A hole in its head, the torn body crumpled sideways
- Melted brain leaked out of the corpse like clumps of gray jam
- He clutched at the mangled ruins of his face
- The brain was gone, scooped out like ice cream

# WHAT'S NEXT?

WE'VE COME TO THE END OF THE WORLD—I mean road. Now that you've mastered the basics of writing apocalypse and survival, it's time to move on to more specific goals, but never fear! I've got you covered there too:

- *Writing Dynamite Story Hooks* walks you through how to emotionally hook readers step by step, line by line regardless of genre.

- *Writing Heroes & Villains* covers how to create all kinds of heroes and villains, as well as supporting cast, teams, and minor characters. You'll also learn how to quickly master writing realistic men and women in your fiction.

- *Writing Monsters & Maniacs* takes you into the world of alien and fantasy races, psycho cults and killers, robots, demons, ghosts, mutants, undead, and more! Includes 150 plot ideas, plus lists of magic, psychic, and supernatural strengths and weaknesses.

If you need help describing things—and I do mean anything—than be sure and grab my *Writers' Phrase Books*:

- #1 Horror
- #2 Post-Apocalypse
- #3 Action
- #4 Fantasy
- #5 Fiction (a short series sampler)
- #6 Science Fiction
- #7 Romance, Emotion, and Erotica

Note that the phrase books are intended as standalones, so all but the Romance one repeat a lot of the same action descriptions. You may not need to own more than one or two of these phrase books.

That's all till next time. Thank you for buying my book and I hope to see you again soon.

— Jackson Dean Chase
*Get a free book at*
www.JacksonDeanChase.com

P.S.: If you enjoyed this book, please leave a review to help others on their author journey.

# POST-APOCALYPTIC READING AND WATCH LIST

Ready to get your read on? On this fiction list you'll find classics like *Earth Abides* and *On the Beach*, along with ridiculously fun '80s romps like *Doomsday Warrior* and *Endworld*, all the way up to recent books. I've purposely restricted the fiction list to works from the mid-twentieth century to the present.

While there are older works from the 1800s and early 1900s, such as H.G. Well's *The Time Machine* and Mary Shelley's *The Last Man*, they are beyond the scope of this book.

Note that I've kept vampires, mutants, and other monsters on the regular post-apocalyptic lists, but segregated zombies onto their own.

As for nonfiction, threats and technology can change quickly. That's why I've kept that list short and mostly recent.

## BOOKS (FICTION)

- *After the Rain* by John Bowen (1958)
- *Alas, Babylon* by Pat Frank (1959)
- *All Fool's Day* by Edmund Cooper (2014)
- *Bird Box* by Josh Malerman (2015)

- *The Black Death* by Gwyneth Cravens and John S. Marr (1978)
- *Blindness* by Jose Saramago (1995)
- *The Book of Eli* (2010)
- *A Boy and His Dog* by Harlan Ellison (1969)
- *C.A.D.S. (Computerized Attack/Defense System)* by John Sievert (Series, 1985-91)
- *Cannibal Reign* by Thomas Koloniar (2012)
- *A Canticle for Liebowitz* by Walter M. Miller, Jr. (1964)
- *The Children of Men* by P.D. James (1992)
- *Children of the Dust* by Louise Lawrence (1985)
- *A Choice of Gods* by Clifford D. Simak (1955)
- *The Chrysalids* by John Wyndham (1955)
- *Damnation Alley* by Roger Zelazny (1969)
- *The Dark* by James Herbert (1980)
- *Dark Universe* by Daniel Galouye (1961)
- *Davy* by Edgar Pangborn (1964)
- *The Day of the Triffids* by John Wyndham (1951)
- *Daybreak 2250* by Andre Norton (1952)
- *The Death of Grass* (aka *No Blade of Grass*) by John Christopher (1955)
- *Deathlands* by James Axler (Series, 1986-2015)
- *The Deep* by Nick Cutter (2015)
- *Domain* by James Herbert (1984)
- *Doomsday Warrior* by Ryder Stacy (Series, 1984-1990)
- *The Drowned World* by J.G. Ballard (1962)
- *Down to a Sunless Sea* by David Graham (2007)
- *Earth Abides* by George R. Stewart (1949)
- *Emergence* by David R. Palmer (1984)
- *End Times Alaska* by Craig Martelle (Series, 2016-17)
- *Endworld* by David L. Robbins (Series, 1986-2015)
- *Engine Summer* by John Crowley (1979)
- *Eternity Road* by Jack McDevitt (2009)
- *The Fifth Wave* by Rick Yancey (Series, 2013-2016)
- *Floating Dragon* by Peter Straub (1982)

- *The Fog* by James Herbert (1975)
- *From the Ashes* by William W. Johnstone (Series, 1983-2003)
- *The Gas* by Charles Platt (1968)
- *The Genocides* by Thomas M. Disch (1955)
- *A Gift Upon the Shore* by M.K. Wren (1990)
- *Heiro's Journey* by Sterling E. Lanier (1983)
- *Horseclans* by Robert Adams (Series, 1975-88)
- *The Hot Zone* by Thomas Preston (1995)
- *How to Survive the End of the World as We Know It* by James Wesley Rawles (2009)
- *I Am Legend* by Richard Matheson (1954)
- *Junk Day* by Arthur Sellings (1970)
- *The Kraken Wakes* by John Wyndham (1963)
- *The Last Ranger* by Craig Sargent (Series, 1987-89)
- *The Last Ship* by William Brinkley (2013)
- *The Last War* by Ryan Schow (Series, 2017-present)
- *Level 7* by Mordecai Roshwald (1981)
- *Life as We Knew It* by Susan Beth Pfeffer (2008)
- *The Long Tomorrow* by Leigh Brackett (1955)
- *Long Voyage Home* by Luke Rhineholt (2012)
- *Lucifer's Hammer* by Jerry Pournelle and Larry Niven (1977)
- *Malevil* by Robert Merle (1975)
- *The Marauders* by Michael McGann (Series, 1989-91)
- *The Maze Runner* by James Dasher (Series, 2009-2016)
- *Nature's End* by Whitley Strieber and James Kunetka (1987)
- *Nomad* by Matthew Mather (Series, 2015-17)
- *On the Beach* by Nevil Shute (1957)
- *One Rainy Night* by Richard Laymon (1991)
- *One Second After* by William R. Forstchen (2011)
- *Parasites Like Us* by Adam Johnson (2004)
- *The Passage* by Justin Cronin (Trilogy, 2010-2016)
- *Path to Savagery* by Robert Edmond Alter (1969)
- *Patriots* by James Wesley Rawles (1998)
- *Phoenix* by David Alexander (Series, 1987-88)
- *Planet of the Apes* by Pierre Boulle (1963)

- *The Postman* by David Brin (1985)
- *The Prince in Waiting* by John Christopher (Trilogy, 1983)
- *Rebirth: When Everyone Forgot* by Thomas C. McClary (1951)
- *Riddley Walker* by Russell Hoban (1998)
- *The Road* by Cormac McCarthy (2007)
- *Roadblaster* by Paul Hofrichter (Series, 1987-88)
- *Quake* by Richard Laymon (1995)
- *Quake* by Rudolph Wurlitzer (1974)
- *The Rest Must Die* by Richard Foster (1959)
- *Shiva Descending* by Gregory Benford & William Rotsler (1985)
- *Slow Apocalypse* by John Varley (2012)
- *Some Will Not Die* by Algis Budrys (1978)
- *The Stand* by Stephen King (1978)
- *Storm Rider* by Robert Baron (Series, 1992-93)
- *Swan Song* by Robert R. McCammon (1987)
- *The Strain* by Guillermo del Toro and Chuck Hogan (Trilogy, 2009-11)
- *The Survivalist* by Jerry Ahern (Series, 1981-1990)
- *The Terry Henry Walton Chronicles* by Craig Martelle (Series, 2016-2017)
- *Tomorrow!* by Philip Wylie (1952)
- *Traveler* by D.B. Drumm (Series, 1984-87)
- *Triumph* by Philip Wylie (1963)
- *War Day* by Whitley Strieber and James Kunetka (1984)
- *The Warlord* by Jason Frost (Series, 1983-87)
- *The Wild Shore* by Kim Stanley Robinson (1984)
- *The Wind from Nowhere* by J.G. Ballard (1961)
- *Wizard of the Wasteland* by Jon Cronshaw (Series, 2017)
- *Wool* by Hugh Howey (2012)
- *Year Zero* by Jeff Long (2002)
- *Z is for Zachariah* by Robert C. O'Brien (2007)

## BOOKS (NONFICTION)

- *Armed Professions: A Writer's Guide* by Clayton J. Callahan (2016)
- *Build the Perfect Bug Out Bag* by Creek Stewart (2012)
- *Can I See Your Hands: A Guide To Situational Awareness, Personal Risk Management, Resilience and Security* by Gav Schneider (2017)
- *The Extreme Weather Survival Manual* by Dennis Mersereau (2015)
- *The Emergency Survival Manual: 294 Life-Saving Skills* by Joseph Pred (2015)
- *How to Survive the End of the World as We Know It* by James Wesley Rawles (2009)
- *The Green Beret Survival Guide: For the Apocalypse, Zombies, and More* by Bob Mayer (2012)
- *How to Survive Off the Grid* by Tim MacWelch (2016)
- *Outdoor Life: Hunting & Gathering Survival Manual* by Tim MacWelch (2014)
- *Outdoor Life: The Ultimate Survival Manual* by Richard Johnson (2014)
- *Post-Apocalypse Writers' Phrase Book: Essential Reference for All Authors of Apocalyptic, Post-Apocalyptic, Dystopian, Prepper and Zombie Fiction* by Jackson Dean Chase (2015)
- *The Practical Bushcraft Survival Guide* by Robbie Jones (2016)
- *Prepping For Life* by Grant Cunningham (2017)
- *Put 'Em Down, Take 'Em Out* by Don Pentacost (1988)
- *Science Fiction Writers' Phrase Book* by Jackson Dean Chase (2016)
- *Survival Medicine & First Aid* by Beau Griffin (2016)
- *Survive Now Thrive Later* by Bob Mayer (2016)
- *Survival Hacks* by Creek Stewart (2016)
- *Survival Medicine & First Aid* by Beau Griffin (2016)
- *Ultimate Bushcraft Survival Manual* by Tim MacWelch (2017)

- *Violence: A Writer's Guide* by Rory Miller (2013)
- *Violence of Mind: Training and Preparation for Extreme Violence* by Varg Freeborn (2018)
- *The Worst Case Scenario Survival Handbook* by Joshua Piven and David Borgenicht (1999)
- *Writing Dynamite Story Hooks* by Jackson Dean Chase (2018)
- *Writing Heroes and Villains* by Jackson Dean Chase (2018)
- *Writing Monsters and Maniacs* by Jackson Dean Chase (2018)

## MOVIES

- *10 Cloverfield Lane* (2016)
- *1990: The Bronx Warriors* (1982)
- *2019: After the Fall of New York* (1983)
- *Aftershock* (2012)
- *Air* (2015)
- *Battle: Los Angeles* (2011)
- *Battletruck* (1982)
- *Beneath the Planet of the Apes* (1970)
- *The Birds* (1963)
- *Blindness* (2008)
- *The Blood of Heroes* (1989)
- *A Boy and His Dog* (1975)
- *By Dawn's Early Light* (TV, 1990)
- *Carriers* (2009)
- *Cherry 2000* (1987)
- *Children of Men* (2006)
- *Chosen Survivors* (1974)
- *The Colony* (2013)
- *Contagion* (2011)
- *Damnation Alley* (1977)
- *The Day of the Triffids* (1962)
- *The Day the Earth Caught Fire* (1961)
- *The Day the World Ended* (1955)

- *Dead End Drive-In* (1986)
- *Death Race 2000* (1975)
- *Def-Con 4* (1985)
- *The Divide* (2011)
- *Doomsday* (2008)
- *Edge of Tomorrow* (2014)
- *Escape from New York* (1981)
- *Escape from the Bronx* (1983, aka *Bronx Warriors 2*)
- *Exterminators of the Year 3000* (1983)
- *Goodbye World* (2013)
- *The Handmaid's Tale* (1990)
- *The Happening* (2008)
- *Hardware* (1990)
- *Hell Comes to Frogtown* (1988)
- *The Host* (2013)
- *Independence Day* (1996)
- *Into the Forest* (2015)
- *Invasion of the Body Snatchers* (1956 and 1978 remake)
- *It Comes At Night* (2017)
- *Johnny Mnemonic* (1995)
- *Kingdom of the Spiders* (1977)
- *The Last Man on Earth* (1964)
- *The Last Survivors* (2014)
- *Left Behind* (2000)
- *Legion* (2010)
- *Logan's Run* (1976)
- *Mad Max* (1979)
- *Mad Max 2: The Road Warrior* (1981)
- *Mad Max 3: Beyond Thunderdome* (1985)
- *Mad Max 4: Fury Road* (2015)
- *Malevil* (1981)
- *The Maze Runner* (Series, 2014-18)
- *Melancholia* (2011)
- *Metalstorm: The Destruction of Jared Syn* (1983)
- *Miracle Mile* (1988)

- *The Mist* (2007)
- *Monsters* (2010)
- *The New Barbarians* (1984)
- *No Blade of Grass* (1970)
- *Oblivion* (2013)
- *The Omega Man* (1971)
- *On the Beach* (1959)
- *Open Grave* (2013)
- *Outbreak* (1995)
- *Pacific Rim* (2013)
- *The People Who Own the Dark* (1976)
- *Phase IV* (1974)
- *Plague* (1979)
- *Planet of the Apes* series (1968-73)
- *The Postman* (1997)
- *The Quiet Earth* (1985)
- *A Quiet Place* (2018)
- *Quintet* (1979)
- *Raiders of Atlantis* (1983)
- *The Rapture* (1991)
- *Rats: Night of Terror* (1984)
- *Ravagers* (1979)
- *Right At Your Door* (2006)
- *The Road* (2009)
- *The Seventh Sign* (1988)
- *Skyline* (2010)
- *Snowpiercer* (2013)
- *Soylent Green* (1973)
- *Stake Land* (2010)
- *Steel Dawn* (1987)
- *The Survivalist* (2015)
- *Take Shelter* (2011)
- *Tank Girl* (1995)
- *Testament* (1983)
- *This Is Not a Test* (1962)

- *This Is the End* (2013)
- *Threads* (TV, 1984)
- *Tomorrow, When the War Began* (2010)
- *The Trigger Effect* (1996)
- *Turkey Shoot* (1982)
- *The Ultimate Warrior* (1975)
- *Vanishing on 7th Street* (2010)
- *War of the Worlds* (1953)
- *Warrior of the Lost World* (1983)
- *Warriors of the Wasteland* (1983)
- *Waterworld* (1995)
- *Without Warning* (TV, 1994)
- *The World, the Flesh, and the Devil* (1959)
- *The World's End* (2013)
- *Z for Zachariah* (2015)
- *Zardoz* (1974)

## TELEVISION

- *The 100* (TV, 2014-present)
- *Cordon* (TV, 2016)
- *The Day After* (TV movie, 1983)
- *The Day of the Triffids* (TV miniseries, 1981)
- *Doomsday Preppers* (TV series, 2012-2014)
- *The Handmaid's Tale* (TV, 2017-present)
- *Heatwave!* (TV, 1974)
- *Jericho* (TV series, 2006-2008)
- *The Last Ship* (TV, 2014-present)
- *Planet of the Apes* (TV series, 1974)
- *The Stand* (TV miniseries, 1994)
- *The Strain* (TV series, 2014-2017)
- *Survivors* (TV series, 2008-2010)
- *Where Have All the People Gone?* (TV movie, 1974)

# ZOMBIE READING AND WATCH LIST

To write great survival horror, you need to watch and read a variety of zombie books, film, and TV. As with the post-apocalyptic list, not all of these are classics, but all have something interesting to offer.

- *Autumn* by David Moody (2010)
- *The Awakening* by M.A. Robbins (Series, 2018)
- *Book of the Dead*, edited by John Skipp/Craig Spector (1990)
- *The Boy on the Bridge* by M.R. Carey (2017)
- *Cell* by Stephen King (2006)
- *Dawn of the Dead* by George A. Romero (1979)
- *Day by Day Armageddon* by J.L. Bourne (2009)
- *Deathbringer* by Bryan Smith (2006)
- *Extinction Horizon* by Nicholas Sansbury Smith (Series, 2017)
- *Feed* by Mira Grant (2010)
- *The First Days* by Rhiannon Frater (2011)
- *The Forest of Hands and Teeth* by Carrie Ryan (2009)
- *Flu* by Wayne Simmons (2012)
- *The Girl With All the Gifts* by M.R. Carey (2014)
- *The Last Town* by Stephen Knight (2017)

- *Monster Island* by David Wellington (2004)
- *My Life as a White Trash Zombie* by Diana Rowland (2011)
- *Night of the Living Dead* by John Russo (1974)
- *Patient Zero* by Jonathan Maberry (2009)
- *Plague of the Dead* by Z. A. Recht (Series, 2006-2018)
- *Please Remain Calm* by Courtney Summers (2015)
- *The Reapers Are the Angels* by Alden Bell (2010)
- *Slow Burn* by Bobby Adair (Series, 2013-2016)
- *Slowly We Rot* by Bryan Smith (2015)
- *Still Dead: Book of the Dead 2*, edited by John Skipp and Craig Spector (1992)
- *Star Wars: Death Troopers* by Joe Schrieber (2009)
- *Star Wars: Red Harvest* by Joe Schrieber (2011)
- *This Is Not a Test* by Courtney Summers (2012)
- *The Troop* by Nick Cutter (2014)
- *The Walking Dead* by Jay Bonansinga (Series, 2011-present)
- *World War Z* by Max Brooks (2006)
- *Zombie Fallout* by Mark Tufo (Series, 2014-present)
- *The Zombie Survival Guide* by Max Brooks (2003)

## ZOMBIE MOVIES

- *28 Days Later* (2002)
- *28 Weeks Later* (2007)
- *The Battery* (2012)
- *Battle Girl: The Living Dead in Tokyo Bay* (1991)
- *The Beyond* (1981)
- *Bio Zombie* (1998)
- *Boy Eats Girl* (2005)
- *Braindead* (1990, aka *Dead Alive*)
- *Burial Ground* (1981)
- *Cargo* (2017)
- *Cemetery Man* (1994, aka *Dellamorte Dellamore*)
- *Children Shouldn't Play with Dead Things* (1972)

- *City of the Living Dead* (1980)
- *Colin* (2008)
- *Collapse* (2014)
- *Contracted* (2013)
- *Contracted: Phase 2* (2013)
- *Dawn of the Dead* (1978/2004)
- *Day of the Dead* (1985)
- *The Dead* (2010)
- *The Dead 2: India* (2013)
- *Dead Air* (2009)
- *Dead Heat* (1988)
- *Dead Heist* (2007)
- *Dead Men Walking* (2005)
- *Dead Shack* (2017)
- *Dead Snow* (2009)
- *Deadgirl* (2008)
- *Diary of the Dead* (2007)
- *Extinction* (2015)
- *Fido* (2006)
- *Flight of the Living Dead* (2007)
- *Freaks of Nature* (2015)
- *The Girl with All the Gifts* (2016)
- *Go Goa Gone* (2013)
- *Hell of the Living Dead* (1980)
- *Highschool of the Dead* (Anime Series, 2010)
- *The Horde* (2009)
- *Horror Express* (1972)
- *It Stains the Sands Red* (2016)
- *Juan of the Dead* (2011)
- *Junk* (2000)
- *Land of the Dead* (2005)
- *Let Sleeping Corpses Lie* (1974)
- *Life After Beth* (2014)
- *Maggie* (2015)
- *My Boyfriend's Back* (1993)

- *The Night Eats the World* (2018)
- *Night of the Creeps* (1986)
- *Night of the Living Dead* (1968/1990)
- *Nightmare City* (1980)
- *Pontypool* (2008)
- *Quarantine* (2008, American remake of *[REC]*)
- *Quarantine 2* (2011)
- *Rammbock: Berlin Undead* (2010)
- *[REC]* (2007)
- *[REC]2* (2009)
- *Return of the Blind Dead* (1973)
- *Return of the Living Dead* (1985)
- *Return of the Living Dead Part II* (1988)
- *Return of the Living Dead 3* (1993)
- *The Returned* (2014)
- *The Rezort* (2015)
- *Seoul Station* (Anime, 2016)
- *Severed: Forest of the Dead* (2005)
- *Shaun of the Dead* (2004)
- *Stacy: Attack of the Schoolgirl Zombies* (2001)
- *Survival of the Dead* (2009)
- *Tombs of the Blind Dead* (1972)
- *Train to Busan* (2016)
- *Versus* (2000)
- *Warm Bodies* (2013)
- *What We Become* (2015)
- *World War Z* (2013)
- *Wyrmwood: Road of the Dead* (2014)
- *Zombi 2* (1979, aka *Zombie*)
- *Zombieland* (2009)

## INFECTED "VIRUS MANIAC" MOVIES

- *Matango* (1963, aka *Attack of the Mushroom People*)

- *I Drink Your Blood* (1970)
- *The Crazies* (1973 and 2010 remake)
- *Who Can Kill a Child?* (1976)
- *Blue Sunshine* (1977)
- *Rabid* (1977)
- *The Grapes of Death* (1978)
- *Cannibal Apocalypse* (1980)
- *The Children* (1980)
- *Nightmare City* (1980)
- *Night of the Comet* (1984)
- *Warning Sign* (1985)
- *Primal Rage* (1988)
- *Grindhouse/Planet Terror* (1997)
- *28 Days Later* (2002)
- *Cabin Fever* (2002)
- *The Happening* (2008)
- *Mutants* (2009)
- *Night of the Comet* (1984)
- *The Signal* (2008)
- *Pontypool* (2009)
- *State of Emergency* (2011)
- *Come Out and Play* (2012)
- *Cooties* (2014)
- *Hidden* (2015)
- *The Girl With All the Gifts* (2016)
- *Viral* (2016)
- *The Cured* (2017)
- *Mayhem* (2017)
- *Mom and Dad* (2017)

## TELEVISION (SCRIPTED)

- *Dead Set* (TV series, 2008)
- *Fear Itself* (TV, 2008, "New Year's Day" episode)

- *Fear the Walking Dead* (TV, 2015-present)
- *In the Flesh* (TV, 2013-14)
- *iZombie* (TV series, 2015-present)
- *The Walking Dead* (TV series, 2010-present)
- *Z Nation* (TV series, 2014-present)

## TELEVISION (PSEUDO-DOCUMENTARIES)

- *Deadliest Warrior*, Season Three, Episode 10, Series Finale: "Vampires vs. Zombies" (TV, 2011)
- *Surviving Zombies* (TV, 2012)
- *The Truth Behind Zombies* (TV, 2011)
- *Zombies: A Living History* (TV, 2011)

# ABOUT JACKSON DEAN CHASE

JACKSON DEAN CHASE is a USA TODAY bestselling author and award-winning poet. His fiction has been praised as "irresistible" in *Buzzfeed* and "diligently crafted" in *The Huffington Post*. Jackson's books on writing fiction have helped thousands of authors.

FROM THE AUTHOR: "I've always loved science fiction, fantasy, and horror, but it wasn't until I combined them with pulp thrillers and *noir* that I found my voice as an author. I want to leave my readers breathless, want them to feel the same desperate longing, the same hope and fear my heroes experience as they struggle not just to survive, but to become something more." — JDC

*Get a free book at* www.JacksonDeanChase.com
jackson@jacksondeanchase.com

amazon.com/author/jacksondeanchase
bookbub.com/authors/jackson-dean-chase
facebook.com/jacksondeanchaseauthor
instagram.com/jacksondeanchase
twitter.com/Jackson_D_Chase

THE ULTIMATE AUTHOR'S GUIDE TO

# WRITING DYNAMITE STORY HOOKS

A MASTERCLASS IN FICTION + MEMOIR

## JACKSON DEAN CHASE

USA TODAY BESTSELLING AUTHOR

# WRITING DYNAMITE STORY HOOKS

## INTRODUCTION AND FIRST CHAPTER PREVIEW

"Your first line sells the book. Your last line sells the next book."

— MICKEY SPILLANE, AUTHOR OF KISS ME DEADLY

THE NUMBER ONE WAY to open a genre book is with action, but be careful how you set it up. You can't jump into a fight scene before you introduce your hero. No one knows him, so no one cares what happens to him. So how do you do it?

Announce the action is taking place and place the enemy close, but not too close. This allows you to get your hero's reaction to the danger, providing valuable insight into who they are, where they are, and what they are up to when the action occurs:

Logen plunged through the trees, bare feet slipping and sliding on the wet earth, the slush, the wet pine needles, breath rasping in his chest, blood thumping in his head.

— JOE ABERCOMBIE, THE BLADE ITSELF

This is a prime example of how to open *in media res* (Latin for "in the middle of things"). Who is Logen? We know he's in a forest, struggling to escape, but from what? Let's see how bestselling grimdark fantasy author Joe Abercrombie handles it in his complete opening paragraph:

> Logen plunged through the trees, bare feet slipping and sliding on the wet earth, the slush, the wet pine needles, breath rasping in his chest, blood thumping in his head. He stumbled and sprawled onto his side, nearly cut his chest open on his own axe, lay there panting, peering through the shadow forest.

We learn Logen has an axe, so whatever he's running from is more than he and his weapon can handle. We also pay off the potential danger of his "bare feet slipping and sliding" from the first sentence by making Logen fall in the second. That lets us know Logen is not invincible, nor is he immune to fear or accidents.

Abercrombie has efficiently *humanized* his hero right from the start by showing, not telling. If he'd simply told us Logen was afraid, that would have been lazy writing. Instead, he shows us through internal and external sensory details. The fast, choppy style conveys panic. As a result, readers can empathize with Logen. The only problem is, we don't know much about him. That's where the second paragraph comes in:

> The Dogman had been with him until a moment before, he was sure, but there wasn't any sign of him now. As for the others, there was no telling. Some leader, getting split up from the boys like that. He should've been trying to get back, but the Shanka were all around. He could feel them moving between the trees, his nose was full of the smell of them. Sounded as if there was some shouting somewhere on his left, fighting maybe. Logen crept slowly to his feet, trying to stay quiet. A twig snapped and he whipped around.

This second paragraph tells us everything else we need to know: Logen is the leader of a band of fighting men, and he has not willingly abandoned them, but been split off during a retreat from a superior force. This deepens reader empathy. The hero is not a coward, simply unlucky. Everyone can relate to that.

In the next few paragraphs, Logen is attacked by two of the Shanka and we see how well he fights. But the author does not let this happen before we get a sense of who his hero and his allies are, where they are, and what's going on. That is critical to the success of not only the book, but the author, and why he received reviews like, "You'd never guess that *The Blade Itself* is Joe Abercrombie's first novel. He writes like a natural."

*The Blade Itself* opens with the hero already in motion and the bad guys hot on his tail.

Here's another example, this time from a science fiction perspective:

Death came for him through the trees.

— STEVE PERRY, THE MAN WHO NEVER MISSED

You can't get better than that. In a single, powerful sentence, we know the hero is in a forest and in terrible danger. From there, the author fills us in on what the danger is:

It came in the form of a tactical squad, four people walking three-and-one, the point followed by the tight concave arc; the optimum number in the safest configuration. It was often said the Confed's military was always training to fight the last war and it was true enough, only there had been enough last wars to give them sand or cold or jungle troops as needed. These four were jungle-trained, they wore class-one shiftsuits with viral/molecular computers able to match backgrounds within a quarter second; they carried .177 Parkers, short and brutal carbines which held five hundred rounds of explosive ammo—one man could put down a half-meter-thick tree with two waves of his weapon on automatic. The quad carried heat sensors, com-implants, Doppler gear and personal sidearms; they were the deadliest and best-equipped soldiers the Confed could field and they were good. They moved through the cool rain forest quietly and efficiently, alert for any signs of the Shanda Scum. If something moved, they were going to spike it, hard.

From the second paragraph, we know this is a sci-fi story, we know the "evil empire" is called the Confed, and they have been at war a long time. We also get a sense of the technology available to them and who they are hunting for (rebel scum). All good stuff, but we still don't know who the hero is. That's fine, because Steve Perry skillfully provides that information in the third paragraph:

Khadaji felt the fear in himself, the familiar coldness in the pit of his belly, an old and unwelcome tenant. He had learned to live with it, it was necessary, but he was never comfortable when it came to this. He took a deeper breath and pressed his back harder against the rough bark of the sumwin tree. He practiced invisibility. The tree was three meters thick, they couldn't see him, and even without his confounder gear their directional doppler and heat sensors wouldn't read through that much solid wood. He listened as they moved past him. The soft ferns brushed against the shiftsuits of the quad; the humus of a thousand years made yet softer sounds under their slippers as they walked, but Khadaji knew exactly where they were when he stepped away from the tree.

You can guess what happens next: Khadaji assassinates the entire quad. After all, the name of the book is *The Man Who Never Missed*.

But what if you want to open with your hero *before* the bad guys are actively hunting her? This next example shows how to do that:

The attack came in the hour before dawn. The girl woke to the stench of burning thatch and the sound of her mother screaming. Outside, in the clearing beyond the hut, she heard her father's response, and the clash of iron on bronze. Another man shouted—not her father—and she was up, throwing off the hides, reaching back into the dark behind the sleeping place for her skinning knife or, better, her axe. She found neither. Her mother screamed again, differently. The girl scrabbled frantically, feeling the fire scorch her skin and the sliding ache of fear that was the threat of a sword-cut to the spine. Her fingers closed on a haft of worn wood, running down to the curve of a grip she knew from hours of oil and polish and the awe of youth; her father's boar spear. She jerked it free, turning and pulling the leather cover from the blade in one move. A wash of predawn light hit her eyes as the door-skin was ripped from its hangings and replaced as rapidly by a shadow. The bulk of a body filled the doorway. Dawn light flicker-ed on a sword blade. Close by, her father screamed her name. *"Breaca!"*

— MANDA SCOTT, DREAMING THE EAGLE

In one paragraph, we know the setting is a primitive village under attack, the time, that the hero is a girl named Breaca who is familiar with weapons, and that she is in danger. Note that the enemy doesn't appear until near the end of the first paragraph. Just long enough to give us the details we need to know *before* the violence begins.

You can pull off the same effect in countless situations, even if you don't begin with action. For example, your hero could be about to play the winning hand in an illegal high-stakes poker game when armed robbers bust in and demand the money. That gives your opening the added advantage of misdirection. The reader thinks he's getting a scene about gambling, then you switch to robbery. The hero goes from winner to loser in a heartbeat, gaining reader empathy in the process.

Sometimes, stories begin with the hero witnessing violence without being involved.

We were about to give up and call it a night when somebody threw the girl off the bridge.

They came to a yelping stop overhead, out of sight, dumped her and took off.

It was a hot Monday night in June. With moon. It was past

midnight and just past the tide change. A billion bugs were vectoring in on us as the wind began to die.

It seemed to be a very final way of busting up a romance.

— JOHN D. MACDONALD, DARKER THAN AMBER

There are a ton of questions raised by this intro:

1. Who is the girl?
2. Is she dead or alive?
3. Who threw her off the bridge?
4. *Why* did they throw her?
5. What were the hero and his friend about to give up before they saw the girl thrown from the bridge?

The arrival of enemies doesn't have to bring with it immediate violence. It can merely be the *threat* of violence, the intimidation, indignity, and humiliation enemies bring.

My used bookstore had been open for just about a month when the police showed up. I hadn't called them, of course; a black man has to think twice before calling the cops in Watts. They came to see me late that afternoon. Two well-built young men. One had dark hair and the other sported freckles.

The dark one wandered around the room, flipping through random books, looking, it seemed, for some kind of contraband.

"Where'd you get all these books, son?" the other cop asked, looking down on me.

I was sitting in my favorite swivel chair behind the makeshift table-desk that I used for book sales and purchases.

"Libraries," I replied.

"Stole 'em?" the dark-haired cop asked from across the room. There was an eager grin on his face.

— WALTER MOSLEY, FEARLESS JONES

There are no swords, no lasers, and nobody's dead (yet) but the threat is real. Menace hangs in the air: menace, bigotry, and hate. The cops are looking to roust the hero just because he's black, and maybe they're looking to do something more besides. A frightening situation, but a fantastic way to hook readers.

But what if it's not action with enemies, but with a natural disaster or some other dangerous survival situation? What do you do then? Pretty much the same thing:

I was thrown out of bed.

— RUDOLPH WURLITZER, QUAKE

It doesn't get simpler than that! The author isn't fooling around and has no intention of wasting our time. He just jumps right in, and that's fine because there's only the hero to focus on and a disaster he can't do anything about. The rest of the opening continues the danger:

The mirror fell off the wall and shattered over the dresser. The floor moved again and the ceiling sagged towards me.

The first paragraph establishes the bedroom and the danger. The second expands the setting and the action, as well as the strange, deadpan reaction the hero has. This tells us we're dealing with a potentially unreliable narrator.

It was dawn and I was in the Tropicana Motel in Los Angeles. There was another trembling through the room and what sounded like wires snapping and windows breaking. Then it was very quiet. I lay back on the floor and shut my eyes. I was in no hurry. There was a high prolonged scream by the pool and then a splash and another, shorter scream. I stood up and raised my arms over my head and tried to touch my toes, an early morning ritual I never perform. The wall next to the bed was moving as if it was alive and I walked into the bathroom.

Another kind of hero would react to in a different manner with the expected panic or bravery. But Wurlitzer isn't interested in normal. His hero does the opposite of what any sane person would do, and that's what makes him interesting. He doesn't care if he lives or dies. Maybe a post-quake world is better than the one before...

Comedy can also work with action to hook readers:

> My sister threw down the book she was reading. To be exact, she threw it at me.
>
> — ROBERT E. HOWARD, "THE LITTLE PEOPLE"

Thrown objects are funny, but what about thrown people?

> They threw me off the hay truck about noon.
>
> — JAMES M. CAIN, THE POSTMAN ALWAYS RINGS TWICE

Action doesn't have to be violence or fast motion; it can be almost any criminal act:

> He always shot up by TV light.
>
> — JAMES ELLROY, AMERICAN TABLOID

Action can imply guilt (or protestations of innocence):

> The building was on fire, and it wasn't my fault.
>
> — JIM BUTCHER, BLOOD RITES

Action can show illness or injury:

> As Roy Dillon stumbled out of the shop, his face was a sickish green, and each breath he drew was an incredible agony.

— Jim Thompson, The Grifters

Opening with someone hurt, sick, or dying creates sympathy and excitement. Readers become invested in the outcome and want to find out how it happened.

Action can also show surprise and instantly reveal genre:

I was staring out the classroom window when I spotted the flying saucer.

— Ernest Cline, Armada

Action can also represent a flurry of activity, even if centered around a seemingly normal event:

As the clock ticked down on her senior year in high school, Laurel McBane learned one indisputable fact.

Prom was hell.

— Nora Roberts, Savor the Moment

Let's come full circle and end this chapter as it began—with violence, but not just any violence. The difference here is the violence is resolved *before* the first sentence:

After the guy was dead and the smell of his burning flesh was off the air, we all went down to the beach.

— Stephen King, "Night Surf"

What kind of sick weirdos would burn a guy to death then go party? If you want to find out, you have to read more, and Stephen King knows that. The rest of his paragraph neatly segues into casually talking about the narrator's friends—normal teenage stuff—but all is not as it seems and the narrator drops clues about a world-ending plague which means there was a good reason to burn that guy after all!

Other than shock value, the advantage to this opening is combining action with mystery. Burning the body creates the action, while the follow-up creates the mystery. Which leads us to the first story secret:

## STORY SECRET #1

COMBINING DIFFERENT OPENINGS

Combining different ways to open your story can create all kinds of interesting results. It's an advanced technique, but when you get it right, it's just as valid a way to open as any of the ten ways on their own—perhaps even more so.

Go back and look at the excerpts in this chapter. Notice they didn't just hook with action, but with mystery, like Stephen King did in "Night Surf." Who is Logen running from? What threw the narrator out of bed? Why is Roy Dillon sick? It's a one-two punch!

*Like where I'm going with this?*
*There are six more successful ways to start your novel*
*and I reveal them all in*
— WRITING DYNAMITE STORY HOOKS —
BY
JACKSON DEAN CHASE
*available in eBook and Paperback*

# WRITING
# HEROES
# &VILLAINS

## A MASTERCLASS IN GENRE FICTION

# JACKSON DEAN CHASE

# WRITING HEROES & VILLAINS

SNEAK PREVIEW OF THE FIRST CHAPTER

"Perfect heroines, like perfect heroes, aren't relatable, and if you can't put yourself in the protagonist's shoes, not only will they not inspire you, but the book will be pretty boring."

— CASSANDRA CLARE, AUTHOR OF THE MORTAL INSTRUMENTS

EVERY HERO SHOULD BE LIKABLE in some way, or at least interesting. To do that, your hero needs to display some measure of wit and charm, as well as enough willpower to stand up to the villain. But heroes can't be perfect. They must be flawed, or risk becoming boring. That's the difference between Batman and Superman.

Batman's got all kinds of flaws, Superman's perfect. Which one sells more copies and puts more butts in seats? Batman. You can't fix perfect. It will always ring false to give Superman issues after he's already been established as perfect (and perfectly boring) for decades. Now if Batman overcomes a flaw, fans will be proud of him, but they won't get bored because they know he'll never be perfect, no matter how hard he tries.

Blowing up the Death Star or teaching an uptight town how to dance are all well and good. This outer journey is the main plot, the story arc that changes the world (or some small part of it). It's also the initial reason people buy into your story, but it's not what truly satisfies them. What they really want to see are heroes who struggle to change themselves in relation to their outer journey.

To do this, every hero needs an inner journey. They get one by facing down their flaws—this constitutes the character arc which makes up the emotional subplot. The success or failure of the character arc sets the tone for the story arc. Let me say that again:

**The success or failure of the character arc sets the tone for the story arc.**

It's the difference between the bittersweet tragedy of *Butch Cassidy and the Sundance Kid* and the joyful triumph of *Star Wars, Episode IV: A New Hope*. Butch and Sundance struggle to change and fail, so they must die (albeit in a blaze of glory). Luke Skywalker and Han Solo struggle to change and succeed, so they live and triumph and go on to have other adventures in a galaxy far, far away.

Note that "live or die" can simply mean "win or lose." Some losers get a second chance in the sequel. For example, Rocky Balboa loses the big boxing match to Apollo Creed at the end of *Rocky*, but beats him in *Rocky II*, and guess what? It's twice as satisfying for Rocky and the audience. If Rocky had failed to beat Creed a second time, the audience would have been justifiably angry at both Rocky and the screenwriter. The whole sequel would have been pointless!

That's not to say that you can't have a chronic "loser" continue his adventures (see The Catalyst Hero, below), but he must be a true underdog people can root for. And because he rarely changes (or needs to), that means he must change the lives of those he comes into contact with for the better. He helps others succeed at their story and character arcs, but ends up alone and riding off into the sunset at the end (as in *Mad Max: Fury Road*).

Eventually, this type of hero must complete his overarching story and character arc, and he should do so successfully. After all, he's suffered so long, he deserves it and the audience demands it. In most cases, this ends the series, so if you're not ready to end it, you should give your underdog glimmers of hope every so often instead—both to remind him and the audience what's at stake in the bigger picture.

While it's generally accepted wisdom that when the hero's inner journey fails, the outer one does too (and vice versa), that's not always the case. There are exceptions where succeeding at an inner journey could mean the hero no longer cares to succeed on his outer journey.

For example, consider the tough jock who passes his prom king crown to the lonely outcast because it means more to the outcast than it ever will to him. He's learned this the hard way over the course of the story, overcoming his arrogant jock flaws in the process. So by the end, he's not only willing to sacrifice outer success for inner success, he *must* do it, or he won't be able to live with himself.

The jock has changed and grown as a person, and so his original outer journey no longer holds meaning to him—but helping the outcast does, and that becomes his new one. The best part is this helps the outcast complete his inner and outer journey as well. The outcast no longer can fail to hide behind excuses of "nobody likes me" and "all jocks are jerks." If you've done your job right, and written the jock and outcast as realistic, flawed characters who we can empathize with, then you've written a winner.

$\approx$

Want to read more?
*Then you need*
THE ULTIMATE AUTHOR'S GUIDE TO
WRITING
HEROES & VILLAINS
*available in eBook and paperback*

Watch for more fantastic writing advice books by
USA TODAY bestselling author
JACKSON DEAN CHASE

# SPECIAL FREE BOOK OFFER

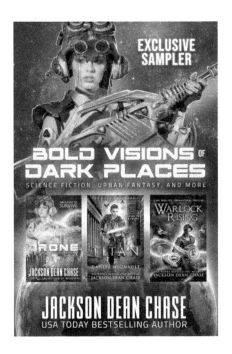

BOLDLY GO WHERE NO BOOK HAS GONE BEFORE

## — FREE EXCLUSIVE SAMPLER —

*"BOLD VISIONS of DARK PLACES"*

featuring the best new sci-fi, urban fantasy, and more

by USA TODAY bestselling author

JACKSON DEAN CHASE

*Get your free book now at*

www.JacksonDeanChase.com

Printed in the USA
CPSIA information can be obtained
at www.ICGtesting.com
LVHW040259281123
765135LV00039B/782